Greenhill Books

USAF COLORS AND MARKINGS IN THE 1990s

USAF COLORS AND MARKINGS IN THE 1990s

DANA BELL

Greenhill Books, London
Presidio Press, California

This edition of *USAF Colors and Markings in the 1990s* first published 1992
by Greenhill Books, Lionel Leventhal Limited,
Park House, 1 Russell Gardens, London NW11 9NN
and
Presidio Press, P.O. Box 1764, Novato, Ca.94948, U.S.A.

British Library Cataloguing in Publication Data
Bell, Dana
USAF colors and markings in the 1990s.
I. Title
358.4183

ISBN 1-85367-112-6

Library of Congress Cataloging-in-Publication Data available

In reproducing in facsimile material from TO 1-1-4,
where there are imperfections in the type or drawings
in this Government publication these have also been reproduced.
Hence the quality of this book sometimes falls short
of normal publication standards.

Quality printing and binding by Butler & Tanner Limited,
Caxton Road, Frome, Somerset BA11 1NF, England.

CONTENTS

INTRODUCTION

As a student of military color schemes, I find that the first two years of this decade have been as evolutionary as any in USAF history. I have long contended one must understand the chain of command to make any sense of aircraft colors and markings; the USAF chain of command is about to experience its most dramatic revisions since 1946. MAC will be replaced by Air Mobility Command, and SAC and TAC will merge into Air Combat Command. How this will effect USAF color schemes remains to be seen, but consider some of the possibilities:

- One month ago, SAC announced plans to repaint all tankers overall Dark Ghost Gray; two weeks ago MAC announced a different mono-chromatic gray scheme to be used on its heavy aircraft; last week the Air Force announced that most tankers would be operated by Air Mobility Command.

- SAC units have been using tail markings which graphically represent some aspect of the unit's history or station; TAC units identify their aircraft with two-letter tail codes. So far, TAC assets transferred to TAC have assumed TAC codes. Under a joint command one or both style marking may be used, or a third style may emerge.

Many readers will recognize Technical Order 1-1-4 ("one dash one dash four") as the source of much of the material in this book. The current version was published in March 1978, with the 36th Revision dated 1 March 1991. I have re-edited the text for commonality (the abbreviation of "technical order," for example, had previously appeared as "TO," "T/O," "to," and "T.O."). My contextual changes and additions are all marked with [brackets].

TO 1-1-4 was not written for the historian, spotter, or modeler, and many important color schemes have been omitted. All added drawing and data (including Appendixes G an H) are drawn from official sources. Again, these additions will be marked with [brackets]. The color chips at the end of the book are matched to FS 595b, with the exception of the Boeing colors provided by the 89th Airlift Wing.

The assembly of this material was made possible by the assistance of many within the Air Force. I am grateful to Major Andy Bourland of SAF/PA, MSgt Roger Ball (89th AW), Maj Paul B. "Bic" Berney (DCANG), Sgt Robert R Brown (89th AW), Sgt. Collins (AFSOC/PA), MSgt Alan Dockery (SAC/PA), Sgt Mark Johnson (MAC/PA), MSgt Chuck Jones (MAC/PA), Maj David Lamp (MAC/PA), Alwyn T "Al" Lloyd of Boeing, Jacque Matthews (WR-ALC), Sgt Hallie Townsend (89th AW/PA), and Lt Col Francis J. Urben (AFSOC/PA).

I also wish to thank Geoffrey (athlete, student, modeler, and son) who brought sandwiches while I pounded the keyboard and, as always, my loving wife Susan. My last note is a thanks to Colleen (the fine young lady and daughter to whom this book is dedicated) who helped with line editing.

Arlington, Virginia
September 1991

SECTION I

GENERAL

1-1. PURPOSE. The purpose of this technical order is to standardize the painting and marking configuration of exterior surfaces of all Air Force aircraft. Also prescribed are limited internal markings that are common among Air Force aircraft. (Applicable weapon system handbooks contain peculiar markings.) Only the types and colors of paints, coatings, finishes, insignia, and markings specified herein will be used on USAF aircraft. This technical order also specifies the authorized identification and function codes for aircraft tubing, pipe lines, hoses, and rigid electrical conduit.

1-2. DEFINITIONS. The following are definitions of terms used when dealing with the painting and marking of USAF aircraft.

a. <u>Air Force Standard Exterior Finish.</u> This term applies to the type and color of the final top coating authorized and required by this technical order for application to the exterior surfaces of noncamouflaged USAF aircraft. This term does not include any of the markings or insignia usually applied over the final top coating or finish. (See Section II.)

b. <u>Air Force Standard Camouflage Finish.</u> Refers to the vari-colored and/or irregular-shaped exterior patterns approved for the camouflage painting of designated aircraft. The colors and patterns used are generally determined by the geographical region of the world in which aircraft are to operate and/or the operational role of the aircraft. This term does not include any of the markings or insignia usually applied over the final top coating or finish.[1] (See Section V.)

c. <u>Special Purpose Exterior Finish.</u> Refers to final coatings of approved paints or lacquers applied to specific portions of aircraft exteriors to provide for special needs. (See Section II.)

d. <u>USAF Standard Markings.</u> These markings that are mandatory for display on all USAF aircraft. (See Paragraph 1-11, Section III, and Section VI.)

e. <u>Special Purpose Markings.</u> Special purpose markings are exterior aircraft markings (other than the USAF standard markings) which are required for appli-

cation or may be authorized under certain circumstances, as stated in this technical order. Special purpose markings are varied in type and usage. They include various insignia, emblems, and symbols, whose need may vary with the differences in weapon system configuration and other pertinent circumstances. (See Section IV.)

f. <u>Aircraft Unit Identification Markings.</u> Alphabetic letters, numerical digits, or combinations of both, that may be displayed on both sides of vertical fins of designated combat and combat support aircraft primarily to allow ready air-to-air recognition. The use of these markings is rigidly controlled and their indiscriminate or arbitrary use is prohibited. (See Section IV.)

g. <u>Tubing, Hose, and Pipe Markings.</u> Those colors, symbols and legends installed on aircraft tubing, hoses, pipe, and rigid electrical conduit to identify the function, content, hazard, or direction of flow. (See Section VII.)

1-3. APPLICABILITY. This technical order is applicable to all USAF, Air National Guard, and Air Force Reserve aircraft. (See Paragraph 4-9.)

1-4. RESPONSIBILITIES.

a. <u>Scope.</u> WR-ALC/MMTRDC[2] is responsible for the contents of this technical order, its currency, and its application within the scope of pertinent Air Force regulations, specifications, and standards. Unless specified elsewhere herein, all matters relating to the painting and marking of aircraft will be directed to WR-ALC/MMTRDC.

b. <u>Authority.</u> AFLC/LOA is the reviewing authority and has final authority for this technical order and all unusual matters relating to the contents of this technical order for which WR-ALC requires guidance, assistance or direction.

c. <u>Compliance.</u> AFLC System Managers (SMs) shall be responsible for assuring compliance to the requirements of AFR 66-34[3]. General Air Force policies promulgated by HQ USAF/LEY under authority of AFR 66-34

---

1. [Despite the official "multi-color" definition, the Air Force is now applying several monochromatic camouflages.]

2. [A list of Air Force organizational abbreviations used in this tech order appears in the glossary on page 139.]

3. [Other relevant regulations, specifications, and tech orders are listed beginning on page 10.]

with respect to the management and control of painting, paint schemes, and markings are included in this technical order.

d. <u>Maintenance and Application.</u> Major commands and using organizations are responsible for maintenance of coatings, finishes, insignia, and markings required by this technical order for all assigned aircraft, and for complete overcoating or strip and repaint of assigned aircraft listed in Table 3 of TO 00-25-4. When work required to comply with this technical order is beyond the capability of the using organization, and upon certification of the major command in accordance with Paragraph 2, TO 00-25-107, AFLC may assume responsibility for such requirement if depot resources are available. AFLC shall, in accordance with the criteria of this technical order, be responsible for complete overcoating or strip and repaint of aircraft listed in Tables 1 and 2 of TO 00-25-4.

1-5. MAJOR COMMAND REGULATIONS. Major commands shall prepare regulations pertaining to the painting and marking of their respective aircraft except as follows:

a. <u>Limitations.</u> These regulations will supplement this technical order and will be limited to distinguishing insignia, markings, and finishes peculiar to their assigned aircraft and as authorized by this technical order.

b. <u>Coordination.</u> Each major command shall coordinate its proposed painting and marking regulation with WR-ALC/MMTRDC prior to publication, distribution, or implementation. These regulations will be carefully reviewed by AFLC to insure that they contain no deviations from the instructions and intent of this technical order.

NOTE

Each major command shall forward published copies of approved painting and marking regulations to Headquarters AFLC/LOAC, WR-ALC/MMTRDC, and the applicable prime aircraft SM listed in TO 00-25-115.

1-6. AUTHORIZED DEVIATIONS. Special missions and/or aircraft assignments require deviation from the standard exterior paint and marking configuration. In all cases WR-ALC will maintain copies of drawings and color photographs (when available) of paint and marking schemes of special mission aircraft.

NOTE

In the event of required painting or marking changes, the using command is responsible to forward the appropriate drawings and photographs to WR-ALC/MMTRDC and the responsible aircraft System Manager.

a. <u>89th Airlift Wing and the 1st Helicopter Squadron.</u>[4] Deviations form the standard exterior paint and marking configurations specified herein, are authorized for aircraft assigned to the 89th Airlift Wing (Special Mission-MAC) and the 1st Helicopter Squadron. Painting and marking of these aircraft will be as specified and approved by Headquarters USAF/LEYY.

b. <u>Energy Research and Development Agency (ERDA).</u> AFSC and MAC aircraft assigned in direct support of the ERDA in nuclear research will be painted as required for the safe accomplishment of that mission. AFSC, MAC, and AFLC (WR-ALC/MMTRDC) will coordinate on the type of paint and paint scheme required. This provision is applicable only to those aircraft that actively engage in required ERDA tests and not to administrative support aircraft.

c. <u>U.S. Air Force Aerial Demonstration Squadron "The Thunderbirds."</u> Special paint scheme and markings are authorized for aircraft assigned to the Air Force Aerobatic Team and will be approved by Hq USAF/LEYY.

d. <u>58th Military Airlift Squadron.</u>[5] Aircraft assigned to the 58th Military Airlift Squadron are authorized aircraft radio call numbers on each side of vertical stabilizers, the American flag, and "United States of America" markings, with no other external USAF identification markings authorized (i.e., "USAF," stars and bars on wings or fuselage, identity of aircraft or fuel under pilot's window, organizational markings). Deviations from standard exterior paint and marking configurations specified herein, are authorized for aircraft assigned to the 58th Military Airlift Squadron. Painting and marking of these aircraft will be as specified and approved by Headquarters USAF/LEYY.

---

4. [On 12 July 1991 the 89th MAW and the 1776th ABW (both at Andrews AFB, Maryland) merged to form the 89th AW. The wing's three flying squadrons are the 1st and 99th Airlift Squadrons and the 1st Helicopter Squadron. The wing's best-known regular passenger is the President; the "Air Force One" aircraft are among the unit's assets.]

5. [The 58th MAS is MAC's special mission unit assigned to the 608th MAG, 322d ALD, in Europe. The squadron's C-12s, C-20s, C-21s, C-135s, UH-1Ns, and T-43s are based at Ramstein AB, Germany, in support of USAFE.]

e. <u>USAFE - C-9A Aeromed Aircraft.</u> C-9A aeromed aircraft assigned to USAFE are authorized aircraft radio call numbers on each side of vertical stabilizer, Red Cross on vertical stabilizer, American flag, and "United States of America" markings.

f. <u>Det 2, 67 ARRS, Special Mission, MAC.</u>[6] UH-1N aircraft assigned to MAC Det 2, 67 ARRS, Special Mission, are authorized radio call numbers on each side of the tailboom, the American flag, and "United States of America" markings. No other MAC, ARS, SAR, or USAF external markings are authorized.

1-7. AIRCRAFT RECEIVED FROM OTHER SERVICES. When types and models of aircraft not previously in the USAF inventory are acquired from other military departments, the respective System Manager shall request from WR-ALC/MMTRDC drawings for the USAF Standard Markings for the new vehicles. The SM will insure that the proper exterior painting and marking configuration of these aircraft is in accordance with the approved drawings.

a. The SM is responsible for the preparation of proposed Special Purpose Markings for servicing, personnel instructions, caution, safety, etc. as specified in Section IV. The SM will forward to WR-ALC/MMTRDC for approval, two sets of exterior drawings illustrating the location of the utility markings on these aircraft by structural member station number and water line (W/L) reference points specifying dimensions and colors to be used.

1-8. REQUEST FOR WAIVERS. Requests for waivers to provisions of this technical order will be limited to those proposed changes based on functional, operational, or special requirements and will contain full written justification, and, where applicable, definitive drawings. Requests for waivers based solely upon appearance will not be approved.

NOTE

Requests for approval of waivers to provisions of this technical order shall be carefully reviewed at each respective command level and, if approved, will be forwarded to WR-ALC/MMTRDC, with the information copy to the System Manager. Where necessary MMTRDC will coordinate with the SM.

1-9. SERVICE TESTS. Requests for authority to test paint type materials on in-service aircraft and/or external components will be forwarded to WR-ALC/MMTRDC for approval. Approved service test programs will be implemented by a coordinated effort, monitored by the appropriate engineering function, the requesting activity, and the pertinent System Manager.

1-10. REPORTING PAINTING AND MARKING DEFICIENCIES. Inadequacies of instructions or deficiencies of specified materials contained in this technical order or other recommended changes will be reported to WR-ALC/MMEDT on AF TO Form 22, Technical Order System Publication Improvement Report, in accordance with TO 00-5-1.

1-11. DECALCOMANIA (DECALS). Decals may be used in lieu of paint for external and internal markings and insignia required by this manual where the contact surfaces are of sufficient smoothness to permit good adhesion. See TO 1-1-8 for instructions for installation and removal of decals.

NOTE

For the purpose of this technical order, decals are defined as specially prepared film containing design, words, or numerals of polyester film, MIL-P-38477, which may be transferred and permanently attached to aircraft or other Air Force equipment.

a. <u>Requisitioning Procedure for Decals.</u> Decal markings required for Air Force equipment and listed in technical manuals under Illustrated Parts Breakdowns, will be requisitioned on Air Force Form 764A in accordance with AFR 6-1 from the appropriate ALC or Air Force depot as indicated in TO 00-25-115.

b. <u>Standard Decals.</u> Decals for the following will be manufactured, stored, and issued by SM-ALC/PDO:

(1) National Star Insignia. (See Appendix A)

(2) "USAF" Marking. (See Appendix A)

(3) "U.S. AIR FORCE" Marking. (See Appendix A)

(4) Aircraft Serial Numbers. (See Appendix A)

(5) Radio Call Numbers. (See Appendix B)

---

6. [The 67th ARRS at RAF Woodbridge was reorganized as the 21st SOS (with MH-53s) and the 67th SOS (with MC-130s) on 3 June 1988. On 1 August 1989 the assets of the Air Rescue and Recovery Service were taken over by the new Air Rescue Service. On 22 May 1990 the ARS' special operations units were transferred to the newly formed Air Force Special Operations Command. Det 2's aircraft and mission were assumed by the 58th MAS (see Paragraph 1-6d).]

(6) American Flag Markings. (See Appendix C)

(7) Armament Placards. (See Appendix E)

(8) Standardized Grounding Marking. (See Appendix E)

c. Non-standard Decals. Decals for non-standard Air Force markings such as command or squadron insignia may be purchased locally in accordance with AFR 6-1 (See Paragraph 12.)

1-12. APPLICABLE REFERENCES. Additional instructions and directives applicable or allied to the application and maintenance of finishes and markings of aircraft are contained in the following:

a. TO 00-25-107, AFLC Maintenance Technical Assistance to Air Force Field Activities.

b. TO 00-25-115, AFLC Maintenance Engineering Prime ALC and AF Depot.

c. TO 00-25-116, Maintenance Responsibilities of AFLC Organizations in Overseas Theaters.

d. TO 00-110-1, Decontamination (TMs-220).

e. TO 00-110N-5, Radioactive Decals, Removal from aircraft parts and equipment.

f. TO 1-1-691, Aircraft Weapons Systems Cleaning and Corrosion Control.

g. TO 1-1-8, Application of Organic Coatings (Paint and Allied Materials).

h. TO 1-1-25, Inspection of Fabric-Covered Surfaces.

i. TO 1-1A-11, Engineering Handbook Series for Aircraft Repair - Fabric Repair and Doping.

j. TO 42A-1-1, Safety, Fire Protection & Health Promotion Aspects of Painting, Doping, and Paint Removal.

k. AFR 900-3, Use and Display of Air Force Flags, Guidons, Streamers, and Automobile and Aircraft Plates.

l. AFR 6-1, Decalcomanias and Other Markings.

m. AFR 66-34, Painting and Marking - Aircraft, Missile, and Drone Exteriors.

n. AFR 82-1, Designating, Redesignating, and Naming of Military Aircraft, Rockets, and Guided Missiles.

o. AFR 400-44, Corrosion Prevention/Control Program.

p. AFR 900-12, Insignia for Winners of USAF Fighter Weapons Meet.

q. Military Specification MIL-M-25047, markings for Airplanes, Airplane Parts, and Missiles (Ballistic Missiles Excluded).

r. Military Specification MIL-M-25165, Aircraft Emergency Escape System, Identification of.

s. Military Standard MIL-STD-1247, Identification of Pipe, Hose, and Tube Lines for Aircraft, Missile, and Space Systems.

t. Military Standard MS33739 (ASG), Aircraft Servicing and Precautionary Markings.

u. Military Specification MIL-F-7179. Finishes and Coatings, General Specification for Protection of Aerospace Weapon Systems, Structures, and Parts.

v. Air Standardization Coordinating Committee Air Standard II/ID for Servicing and Ground Handling Codes.

w. CENTO STANAG #3230 - Emergency Marking on Aircraft.

x. NATO STANAG #3109 - Servicing and Ground Handling Codes.

y. NATO STANAG #3230 - Emergency Marking on Aircraft.

SECTION II

STANDARD EXTERIOR FINISHES FOR

USAF AIRCRAFT

2-1. METAL EXTERIOR FINISHES. Metal exterior surfaces of all Air Force aircraft (see policy guidelines in Paragraph 2-2 below), other than those made of titanium and corrosion-resistant steels, require surface protection from the effects of corrosion and therefore will be painted in accordance with the provisions of this technical order.

a. Titanium or Steel. Since titanium or corrosion-resistant steels, when used, make up only a part of the total aircraft exterior surface, they will also be painted with the same finishes as the adjacent metals, providing temperatures permit.

NOTE

Do not paint any equipment where the application of paint will deter its operational capabilities (antenna, radomes, etc.).

b. Treatment of Metal Exteriors. The treatment of metal exteriors for corrosion control is specified in TO 1-1-691. The proper surface preparations for painting, priming, and application of finish coatings are specified in TO 1-1-8. In addition to protective finishes, regular scheduled surface washing and cleaning in accordance with TO 1-1-691 will minimize the probability of corrosion. Some surfaces will require additional surface protection and will be specified further in this section.

2-2. POLICY GUIDANCE. It is a general policy (AFR 66-34) that all Air Force aircraft will be painted as a prime means of corrosion protection and prevention. Inherent in this policy is the responsibility to preserve a professional paint appearance as an integral part of a well-managed corrosion control program (AFR 400-44). The requirement to paint, however, must be tempered with good judgement and in consideration of funds availability. It is not intended that crash programs be established for the prompt painting of aircraft. Aircraft will be painted in accordance with a service life plan unless there is an over-riding operational requirement as determined by HQ USAF/XOO. Aircraft should be scheduled for painting with due regard for other scheduled maintenance and funding. Aircraft are not to be painted unless they are programmed for retention in the active inventory for at least two years after painting. Aircraft will receive maintenance painting to preserve coating integrity. The following criteria will apply in programming aircraft for painting:

a. Aircraft determined to have a sound paint system already applied will not be repainted solely to incorporate color, improve appearance or material changes to the standard paint system and color scheme as listed herein. When it is necessary to perform maintenance on such aircraft with former standard or non-standard paint (unless deteriorated to the extent that complete replacement is required), use like or same-type material as originally applied for maintenance-painting purposes. For new aircraft entering the inventory or for aircraft requiring repainting the cognizant engineering authority (either the AFSC System Program Office or AFLC System Program Manager, depending on PMRT status) in conjunction with the major operating commands will evaluate all available technical, engineering, and historical evidence to determine the appropriate corrosion protection and prevention system (type coating, color schemes, service life criteria, etc.) for each weapons system. A coordinated paint/repaint plan will be developed and kept current for each weapon system. This plan may be based on a weighted paint program inspection and evaluation procedure, calendar time/severity zone criteria, or other approved technique. All aircraft under Tables I and II of TO 00-25-4 will be inspected prior to (if possible) and/or during PDM for condition of the paint. The purpose of the inspection will be to determine if the aircraft should be repainted or touched-up.

(1) In determining requirements for sectional overcoating, total overcoating, or strip and repaint, the following general technical criteria should be considered in the development of the approved weapon system paint plan.

(a) Sectional or total overcoat if paint is oxidized, discolored, stained, chipped, scratched, or peeled from primer and the primer is adhering soundly to the aircraft. If this condition is extensive, complete overcoating of the aircraft or section is preferred over spot maintenance painting.

(b) Strip/repaint if the following defects or combination of them exist: areas which have been overcoated (primer plus topcoat) at least three times; primer is not adhering to base metal; or the paint system is peeled to base metal.

(2) When applying the above criteria to determine painting requirements and a combination of defects for overcoating and strip and repaint exists, the following

general economic guidelines should be considered in the development of the approved weapon system paint plan:

(a) When determining sectional or total aircraft overcoating and a combination of defects exists, overcoating may be accomplished if time or manhour requirements for surface preparation (mask, sand, and clean) do not exceed 70% of the time or manhours required for complete strip/repaint.

(b) Sectional stripping may be required, as determined by deteriorated areas, on an aircraft designated to be completely overcoated. Complete overcoating with prior sectional stripping may be accomplished if the combined time or manhours for sectional stripping and surface preparation for overcoat do not exceed 70% of the time required for complete strip/repaint.

(c) Complete strip/repaint should be accomplished in lieu of overcoating whenever time or manhour requirements for masking, sanding, and cleaning for total or sectional overcoating exceed 70% of those to accomplish strip/repaint.

(3) In the absence of an approved tailored weapon system paint plan, the above criteria will apply to all aircraft.

NOTE

For purposes of planning facility requirements, the expected paint system average life before the need for strip/repaint is:

High gloss	- 8 years
Flat (unsheltered)	- 6 years
Flat (sheltered)	- 8 years

NOTE

This assumes good maintenance of the coating system and complete overcoat at approximately the mid-life point.

For the purpose of mission change or other reassignment of aircraft with sound coating systems for which the existing coating or markings are inappropriate, the major command shall overspray the existing paint system in accordance with TO 1-1-8.

b. Maintenance Painting. Maintenance painting procedures will not be used if there is any indication of major failure of the aircraft paint system. Operational environment and life expectancy of the paint system will be considered in making this determination. If major failure of the paint system is evident, complete repaint should be scheduled promptly.

NOTE

Table I and II (TO 00-25-4) aircraft painting should be programmed for accomplishment during a scheduled entry into a depot-level facility for PDM, other modification/maintenance requirements, or whenever corrosion is evident, whichever occurs first. The evidence of corrosion in any case shall mean the point at which corrosion would cease to be controlled in accordance with criteria of technical orders 1-1-691 and/or the system peculiar (-23, etc.) technical orders. Table III (TO 00-25-4) aircraft will be painted by using organizations in accordance with technical orders 1-1-8 and 42A-1-1.

(1) Sectionalized painting of aircraft. To minimize the contrast between new coatings and aged or bleached topcoat finishes, individual aircraft may have sectionalized painting for maintenance purposes. The sections are defined as major sections of the aircraft such as wings, nacelles, stabilizers, rudders, empennage, or other portions as from one major assembly joint to another. This may also be applied to single panels of metal between skin joints, doors, control surfaces, and access panels as applicable. The criteria for aircraft in Paragraph 2-2a will be used to determine requirements for sectionalized painting. Sectionalized painting will be accomplished in lieu of spot maintenance painting when the criteria of Paragraph 2-2a is met. The paint material used must be of the same type as on the adjacent serviceable areas. Smaller portions of deteriorated paint (less than that which qualifies for sectionalized painting), must be touched up with the conventional spot or strip pattern.

NOTE

Under no circumstances will total section/panel areas, which meet the foregoing sectionalizing criteria, be considered as cumulative requirements for total aircraft repaint. Total repaint criteria will apply based upon the total aircraft assessment before the sectionalized concept is applied.

In order to realize the maximum benefits of corrosion protection afforded by painting, it is necessary to achieve proper adhesion of the paint to the metal surfaces or existing coatings on which applied. In this regard, it is Mandatory that all steps of surface preparation and application of coating systems, as specified in TO 1-1-8, be strictly followed.

2-3. AIR FORCE STANDARD EXTERIOR FINISHES. (See Appendix B.) Aliphatic polyurethane coating Specification MIL-C-83286 gray, color number 16473, is the standard Air Force exterior finish coating for all aircraft. This coating will be specified for or used in lieu of Specifications MIL-L-19537, MIL-L-19538, MIL-C-27227, MIL-L-38412, MIL-C-81352, and other specifications for painting or refinishing of all aircraft. The following criteria will apply in converting to the aliphatic polyurethane coating:

NOTE

The F-111A/D/E/F, FB-111A,[7] and EF-111A are exempt from the policy that the standard exterior finish for Air Force aircraft is Specification MIL-C-83286, aliphatic polyurethane. The standard exterior finish for the above aircraft will be epoxy primer, Specification MIL-P-23377, and topcoat, acrylic lacquer, Specification MIL-L-81352.

a. Authorized conversions shall be limited to aircraft or aerospace equipment normally scheduled for complete repainting only.

b. The polyurethane paint will not be specified or used to touch up other types of paint such as acrylic nitrocellulose Specifications MIL-L-19537, MIL-L-19538, etc.

c. Conversion will be limited to aircraft that actually need painting or complete repainting due to deterioration of existing paint finish. Painting for the sole purpose of converting to the polyurethane coating is not approved. (See Paragraph 2-2.)

2-4. EXTERIOR FINISH IDENTIFICATION CODES. Instructions for the application of required code markings depicting the coating system applied to overall aircraft exteriors is contained in Appendix A.

2-5. SPECIAL PURPOSE EXTERIOR SOLAR RESISTANT FINISHES. For the purpose of this technical order, solar resistant finish is defined as a white cap painted on the top surface to reduce the aircraft interior temperature. The solar resistant finish is authorized only for those aircraft used primarily as personnel carriers or that routinely carry heat sensitive equipment as part of their mission. In either case, or for special purpose aircraft, authorization must be provided by the major command and be reflected in the major command regulation.

a. Configuration. Normally, the solar resistant finish

on the top surface of the fuselage shall be separated from the lower adjacent finish by a three-inch blue stripe, color number 15044. For small aircraft equal to and smaller than T-39 aircraft, use a one and one-half inch blue separation stripe. The upper edge of the stripe shall extend parallel to the fuselage reference line from a point approximately tangent to the lowermost edge of the pilot's compartment windows aft to infinity. Aircraft painted with solar resistant finish shall have the vertical tail painted white also. It is permitted to break the continuity of the straight line in the extreme aft section for appearance purposes.

b. Color Specification. The authorized solar resistant paint system is Specification MIL-C-83286 white, color number 17875, for the top of the fuselage and blue, color number 15044 for the separation stripe; if the specific aircraft is authorized for a system other than the aliphatic polyurethane system then the solar resistant finishes shall be compatible with that applied.

NOTE

Unless otherwise specifically authorized in this technical order, no marking or lettering will be applied on the white solar resistant finish on the aircraft fuselage.

2-6. EXHAUST, GUN GAS, AND ROCKET BLAST AREAS. Polyurethane coating system, Specification MIL-C-83286 will be used for the protection of surface areas exposed to engine exhaust, gun gases, or rocket blast.

a. Exhaust Track Areas. Exhaust track areas will normally be painted black, color number 17038. However, grey, color number 16473, or white, color number 17875, may be used when replacing the paint in the affected area and where necessary to retain the original aircraft color scheme.

b. Gun Gas and Rocket Blast Areas. Gun gas and rocket blast areas areas will not require a special color designation other than that of the color of the adjacent aircraft exterior finish. Specific areas requiring such coating will be as prescribed by the respective SM.

2-7. THERMAL REFLECTIVE FINISH. All USAF aircraft programmed to participate in thermonuclear tests normally shall be protected with a thermal reflective finish system to include a topcoating of polyurethane, Specification MIL-C-83286, white, color number 17875. The required paint scheme will be specified by type and model aircraft by WR-ALC. Application instructions are included in TO 1-1-8.

---

7. [SAC has retired its fleet of FB-111As, many of which have been reassigned to TAC as F-111Gs.]

Authorization for applying thermal reflecting finishes will be obtained from WR-ALC/MMTRDC.

2-8. SALT WATER, SALT AIR, AND POLLUTED AIR. Adequate corrosion resistance from salt water spray, salt heavy atmosphere, and various air pollutants is provided by the standard exterior finish, aliphatic polyurethane Specification MIL-C-83286.

2-9. ANTI-GLARE FINISHES. Aircraft surfaces (such as nose section and cowling) which reflect an objectionable glare to the pilot and crew shall be finished with aliphatic polyurethane Specification MIL-C-83286, black, color number 37038, as applicable.

2-10. ACID RESISTANT FINISHES. Specification MIL-C-83286 or TT-L-54 shall be applied to areas susceptible to acid, alkali, and urine corrosion such as battery compartments, buffet, lavatory, and relief tube discharge areas. The area to receive the coating shall be cleaned in accordance with TO 1-1-1 and the coating applied in accordance with TO 1-1-8.

2-11. EXTERIOR FABRIC FINISHES AND FINISH IDENTIFICATION CODES. Exterior fabric parts shall be doped in accordance with TO 1-1A-11. Finish coating will be gray, color number 16473. A record marking of when each fabric surface is recovered or refinished will be stenciled on each fabric surface and each separately replaceable fabric section of a combination metal and fabric covered surface in accordance with instructions contained in Appendix A.

2-12. FINISHES FOR AIRCRAFT PROPELLERS AND HELICOPTER ROTORS. Refer to applicable aircraft, propeller, or rotor technical order for approved blade finishes and blade data markings. (See Section IV for approved propeller and rotor safety markings.)

2-13. ANTI-SKID COATING FOR WALKWAYS. When approved by the appropriate SM, walkway coating conforming to Specification MIL-W-5044 may be applied in colors to contrast or match the adjacent coating, in accordance with TO 1-1-8, on the wing roots of subsonic fixed-wing aircraft on which the wing roots are used as a walk-on area. The coating may also be applied on other areas that receive heavy duty traffic or are hazardous to pilot and service personnel. Generally, the wing-root walkway coating will be applied to both wing roots to a width of 18 inches measured from the fuselage, and shall extend from just aft of the leading edge to just forward of the trailing edge.

2-14. FINISH SYSTEM FOR ENGINE AIR INTAKE DUCTS/SCOOPS. Unless otherwise specified in applicable aircraft technical orders, the finish system for all engine air intake ducts/scoops shall be white, color number 17875. The forward opening of the ducts/scoops shall be coated to blend with the exterior color of the aircraft, i.e. grey for grey aircraft, blue for blue aircraft, camouflage for camouflaged aircraft, etc., to a depth sufficient to ensure that the white cannot be seen from the immediate exterior. The paint system in the ducts/scoops should be inspected and touched up or repainted on the same basis as the exterior system.

STANDARD MARKINGS AND INSIGNIA FOR USAF AIRCRAFT

3-1. GENERAL. The markings and insignia contained in this section will be applied to all Air Force aircraft as specified herein. Section V contains special instructions concerning markings and insignia for camouflaged aircraft. Appendix A reflects specific instructions, dimensions, etc., for the proper application of these markings and insignia.

3-2. USAF STANDARD MARKINGS AND INSIGNIA. The following are the USAF standard markings and insignia for Air Force aircraft.

ITEM	GENERAL LOCATION
National Star Insignia	Wing and Fuselage
"USAF" Marking	Aircraft Wings
"U.S. AIR FORCE" Marking	Aircraft Fuselage
Serial Number	Aircraft Fuselage
Aircraft Data Legend	Aircraft Fuselage
Aircraft Radio Call Number	Aircraft Vertical Fin

NOTE

The above USAF Standard Insignia and Markings will not be altered in location, dimension, or configuration from the specifications reflected herein to accommodate any other insignia or marking.

a. National Star Insignia. The National Star Insignia will be installed on all USAF aircraft. The insignia shall consist of an Insignia White five-pointed star located within an Insignia Blue circumscribed circle. An Insignia White rectangle shall be located on each side of the star. The top edge of the rectangle shall form a straight line with the upper edges of the horizontally opposed star points. An Insignia Red horizontal stripe shall be centered in each end of the rectangle. An Insignia Blue border shall outline the entire insignia. The Insignia Blue border and Insignia Blue circle may be omitted when the National Star Insignia is applied on blue or black finishes. Specific instructions for installing the National Star Insignia and appropriate dimensions are contained in Appendix A.

(1) National Star Insignia on Aircraft Fuselage. The National Star Insignia will normally be applied to each side of the aircraft fuselage, midway between the wing trailing edge and the leading edge of the stabilizer.

(2) National Star Insignia on Aircraft Wings. The National Star Insignia shall be applied on the upper surface of the left wing and on the lower surface of the right wing as applicable.

(3) National Star Insignia on Helicopters. Four National Star Insignia shall be applied on the aircraft fuselage of helicopters. The insignia shall be located so that the insignia will be visible from each side, from above, and from below. Because of helicopter design configuration the insignia shall be located so as to provide maximum identification. Such locations shall be standardized on like model and series helicopters.

b. "USAF" Marking. The marking "USAF" shall be applied on the lower surface of the left wing and the upper surface of the right wing on all USAF aircraft. The lower surface marking shall be omitted when thermal reflective finishes have been applied. The height and location of the marking "USAF" will correspond, if at all possible, with the National Star Insignia applied on the opposite wing. The top of the letters shall be toward the leading edge of the wing.

c. "U.S. AIR FORCE" Marking. The marking "U.S. AIR FORCE" will be applied and maintained on the left and right sides of the fuselage of all aircraft.

d. Serial Number Markings - Aircraft. The aircraft serial number marking is included in the Aircraft Data Legend marking.

e. Data Legend Marking - Aircraft. The Aircraft Data Legend reflects the owning military component, the aircraft type, model and series, aircraft serial number, the grade fuel to be serviced in the aircraft, and the identiplate location within the aircraft. This marking may be located on the left side of the fuselage near the pilot's compartment or near the single point refueling location.

(1) A typical Aircraft Data Legend marking follows:

EXAMPLE:

U.S. AIR FORCE [F-15A]
AF SERIAL NO. [73-091]
SERVICE THIS AIRCRAFT WITH GRADE [JP-4] FUEL
IDENTIPLATE LOCATION [IN DOOR 29]

(2) In the above format, the first entry identifies the owning military service and aircraft type, model, and series. The second line is to be used for the complete aircraft serial number. The next entry is to be used to identify the grade fuel to be serviced in the aircraft, and the last entry reflects the identiplate location.

NOTE

The manufacturer's name and the popular name for an aircraft are specifically prohibited from use or display on any Air Force aircraft.

f. Aircraft Radio Call Numbers. Radio call numbers, in Arabic numerals, will be applied to all USAF aircraft on each side of the vertical stabilizer, or in the case of aircraft with multiple vertical stabilizers, on the outboard side of each outermost vertical stabilizer. For helicopters with no vertical fins, the numbers will be applied to both sides of the fuselage or hull. (See Appendix A for numeral dimensions and locations.)

(1) The aircraft radio call numbers consist of five numerals which are derived from the aircraft serial number. Normally, the last five numerals of the aircraft serial number are used to compose the radio call number. The first numeral of the contract year and the hyphen of the aircraft serial number will not be used in radio call numbers.

EXAMPLES:

The radio call number of an aircraft whose serial number is 63-545143A will be 45143.

The radio call number of an aircraft whose serial number is 62-3467 will be 23467.

(2) In the event five numerals are not available in the aircraft serial number from which to derive the numerals required for the radio call number, the second numeral of the aircraft contract year (omitting the hyphen) shall then be used, followed by necessary quantities of zero to produce five numerals.

EXAMPLE:

The radio call number of aircraft serial number 59-12A would be 90012.

(3) All radio call number placards installed within aircraft, including helicopters, shall reflect the same radio call number as applied on the aircraft exterior.

3-3. GENERAL SPECIFICATION FOR LETTERING AND NUMERALS USED IN MARKINGS FOR AIRCRAFT. Vertical block (Chamfered Gothic) type

letters and Arabic numerals should be used when applying markings on aircraft. (See Appendix A for construction of letters and numerals.) Unless otherwise specified herein, Insignia Blue, color number 15044, will be used for letters and numerals applied on gray or white surfaces. Gloss black, color number 17038, may be used as a substitute for the Insignia Blue. Insignia White, color number 17875, will be used on red finishes. Insignia Red, color number 11136, will be used on black finishes. Use Specification MIL-C-83286 aliphatic polyurethane. Use of decals, both gloss and camouflage, conforming to Specification MIL-P-38477, Type 1, Class 2, are authorized for use in lieu of polyurethane paint. This is a premasked type decal that is applied over the primer and then painted over. The premask material is then removed which leaves all edges of the decal sealed with the topcoat of paint. Touchup and repair of markings and small instructional markings with lacquers Specifications MIL-L-19537 or MIL-L-19538 are authorized.

3-4. IDENTIFICATION OF PAINT SHOP AND THE APPLIED FINISH. All aircraft receiving a paint finish on the exterior surfaces, the contractor or activity performing the work shall apply markings consisting of a circular patch approximately 2-1/2 to 4 inches in diameter. The patch shall be located on the right side of the fuselage, on the underside and even with the leading edge of the horizontal stabilizer or delta wing.

a. This marking shall contain the following information:

(1) Contractor or overhaul activity Federal Manufacturer's code. (If no code exists, name and address.)

(2) Date of completion of paint application (day, month, year).

(3) Identification by specification number of every coating of the general system applied to the exterior of the aircraft.

b. Stencils or approved decals may be used for this marking. Border and letters shall be black, color 17038, for non-camouflaged aircraft and as per Paragraph 5-6 for camouflaged aircraft. (See Figure A-5.)

NOTE

The above marking is a firm requirement and shall not be disfigured or oversprayed during touchup operations. If touchup requires overspraying of this marking, it shall be replaced afterwards.

SECTION IV

SPECIAL PURPOSE MARKING FOR USAF AIRCRAFT

4-1. GENERAL. Unless otherwise specified, the dimensions, colors, and materials required for USAF Standard Markings and Insignia in Section III also apply to Special Purpose Markings. Due to variance in equipment configuration and restrictions in the uses of some markings, Special Purpose Markings may or may not be applicable to all aircraft. However, when applicable and authorized for use, special purpose markings will be applied in the dimensions, colors, and locations as specified herein.

4-2. AMERICAN FLAG MARKINGS. The display of the American Flag Marking on aircraft exteriors is intended for specific uses which have national significance or U.S. diplomatic connotation. As such, the use of the flag marking will be restricted and approved only by Headquarters USAF/LEYY. The routine or occasional overseas flight of aircraft, the assignment of aircraft to foreign soil, or the intra-theater travel of overseas-based aircraft is not sufficient reason for the use of the American Flag Marking. The National Star Insignia and "USAF" markings painted upon aircraft exteriors in accordance with instructions contained herein, adequately identify these and other Air Force aircraft.

a. American flag markings are authorized for use only on the following aircraft:

(1) Air Attache.

(2) Military Assistance Advisory Group (MAAG).

(3) USAF Mission.

(4) AFSC Apollo[8] Range Instrumentation Aircraft EC-135 (AFSC-ARIA) and NKC-135A S/N 53-3132 (BIG CROW)[9].

(5) 89th Military Airlift Wing, MAC.

(6) MAC airlift forces aircraft.

(7) Air Force Section Mission (U.S. Military Group Aircraft in Latin America).

(8) National Emergency Airborne Command Post [NEACP] E-4 aircraft.

(9) 58th Military Airlift Squadron, USAFE.

(10) ANG and Air Force Reserve airlift aircraft for which MAC is the gaining command.

(11) Det 2, 67th ARRS, Special Mission, MAC.

(12) E-3A aircraft assigned to the 522d AWACW[10].

(13) EC/RC-135 aircraft.

b. The American Flag Marking, when authorized, shall be located on both sides of the rudder or vertical stabilizer above all other markings of significance. The flag shall be positioned horizontally and in such a manner that the union shall be uppermost. The bars of the flag shall appear to be trailing at all times. (See Appendix C.)

c. The following standard sizes are specified for American Flag Markings used on USAF aircraft:

(1) 19 x 36 inches.

(2) 21 x 40 inches.

(3) 25 x 48 inches.

(4) 31.4 x 60 inches.

NOTE

The flag or national insignia/emblem of any country, other than the United States of America, will not be displayed on any USAF aircraft for any reason.[11]

---

8. [The dish-nosed Apollo Range Instrumentation Aircraft were renamed Advanced Range Instrumentation Aircraft in the mid-1970s. Three ARIA EC-135Ns now share their mission with four similar EC-18Bs, all assigned to AFSC's 4950th Test Wing.]

9. ["Big Crow" is the code name for an NKC-135E (as redesignated with new engines in January 1991) assigned to HQ SAC at Offut AFB, Nebraska. The actual serial number is 55-3132.]

10. [All USAF E-3As have been converted to E-3Bs and E-3Cs. They are all assigned to the 552d (not the 522d) AWACW.]

11. [Well, actually, there are two reasons: (1) victory markings dating from Vietnam and the recent Gulf War often display a Soviet star or and Iraqi flag; and (2) the Thunderbirds display the flags of every country where they have performed.]

4-3. "UNITED STATES OF AMERICA" MARKING.

a. The words "UNITED STATES OF AMERICA" are authorized to be painted on fuselage exteriors of the following aircraft authorized the American Flag Marking:

(1) Air Attache.

(2) MAAG.

(3) USAF Mission.

(4) AFSC-ARIA.

(5) 89th Military Airlift Wing, MAC.

(6) Air Force Section Mission (U.S. Military Group Aircraft in Latin America).

(7) National Emergency Airborne Command Post E-4 aircraft.

(8) 58th Military Airlift Squadron, USAFE.

(9) Det 2, 67th ARRS, Special Mission, MAC.

b. When authorized, the marking "UNITED STATES OF AMERICA" will be applied on both sides of the aircraft fuselage, parallel to and above the top of the cabin windows. The fuselage marking "U.S. AIR FORCE" referred to in Paragraph 3-2 will be removed from these aircraft. (See Appendix C.)

4-4. ORGANIZATIONAL INSIGNIA OR EMBLEMS. All proposed organizational emblems or insignia (major command, wing, group, or squadron) for use on aircraft or missiles, must meet the criteria of AFR 900-3 and be approved in accordance with the provisions of that document.

a. Approved organizational emblems or insignia may be placed on non-camouflaged aircraft. The major command headquarters shall be the approving authority for the use of organization emblems on its aircraft and the precise location on the vehicle at which the emblem will be installed. The use and location of the emblem will be contained in the pertinent major command regulation.

b. In all cases, approved organizational emblems to be installed on aircraft shall not exceed 2/3 the size of the fuselage National Star Insignia. Further, standard Air Force markings will not be altered or relocated to accommodate organizational emblems. Emblem locations and dimensions will be the same for similar aircraft types and models. Whenever an aircraft is permanently transferred for active service, the transferring unit will remove its organizational emblems prior to transfer. Aircraft being deactivated or processed for storage may be exempted from the requirement to remove organizational emblems.

4-5. OUTSTANDING UNIT AWARD MARKINGS. A replica of the Outstanding Unit Award ribbon earned by an organization may be installed on the sides of the aircraft fuselage in a suitable location designated by the applicable major air command headquarters. Criteria regarding size and location as stated in Paragraph 4-4 above is applicable except that the length of the marking shall not exceed 12 inches and the length to width ratio will be maintained at 4 to 1, i.e. 12 inches x 3 inches, etc.

4-6. CREW MARKINGS. The names of pilot, crew chief, or other members of the flight/ground crew may be applied to the exterior of camouflaged or non-camouflaged aircraft at the option of the major command.

a. Generally, the names will be applied to the left side of the fuselage (right side for helicopters), near the pilot's window and clearly visible from ground level. On large aircraft such as C-130s, C-135s, C-141s, C-5s, etc., where the names will not be clearly visible from ground level, the names may be placed adjacent to the forward crew/passenger entrance door, when approved by the major command.

b. Block lettering, not higher than two inches, shall be used for the markings. On non-camouflaged aircraft, letters shall be orange-yellow[12], color number 13538, and on camouflaged aircraft the letters shall be tan, color number 30219, on a background block only as large as needed to accommodate the information, 6 inches to 24 inches high, consistent with the size of the aircraft. If the background is presently black, the background block is not required. If the background is gray, the background block is not required, and the letters will be black, color number 37038. Background sizes and lettering should be standardized throughout the unit.

---

12. [The color "orange-yellow" was also listed in TO 1-1-4 as "yellow," "yellow-orange," and "orange." This book uses the more-accurate "orange-yellow."]

c. Examples of the markings are as follows:

PILOT: L/Col. W.B. JONES
CREW CHIEF: SSGT A.B. JOHNSON

or

CREW CHIEF: SSGT A.B. JOHNSON

or

CREW CHIEF
SSGT A.B. JOHNSON

4-7. LOCAL STATION NUMBERS AND MARKINGS FOR AIRCRAFT. Where large numbers of aircraft are assigned to a station, or duplication of the last three digits of aircraft serial numbers occurs on such a station, or where visibility at a station is extremely poor due to snow or dust conditions, the major command may request and the System Manager may authorize the application of local "Station Numbers" as an aid to maintenance and operational control.

a. Station Numbers. The "Station Numbers" will be located on the nose section of fixed wing aircraft and on the deflector shields or other forward component of helicopters, as designated by the particular System Manager. Numerals will not be more than eight inches in height and proportionate to the aircraft size and height. The "Station Numbers" will be removed prior to transfer.

b. Markings. Where large numbers of a similar type of aircraft are assigned to a station in the CONUS, major commands may authorize a distinguishing colored horizontal stripe for application on both sides of the topmost portion of the vertical fin. A different color may be assigned each unit owning such aircraft. These stripes will be appropriately removed by the installing organization when the aircraft is to be transferred.

NOTE

The above horizontal stripes will not be applied over apex antenna on vertical stabilizers, the painting of which would interfere with system operation. In such cases, the six inch stripe will be applied immediately below the antenna on both sides of the vertical stabilizer.

4-8. AIR NATIONAL GUARD (ANG) AIRCRAFT. USAF exterior finishes, insignia, and markings are applicable to ANG aircraft. In addition to standard USAF markings, ANG aircraft may be further marked with the state name, squadron insignia, and state insignia, including the ANG Minuteman decal. These may be obtained by each state in accordance with in-

structions contained in Section I of this technical order.

NOTE

States desiring to affix markings and/or insignia similar to those of their gaining commands will obtain approval from their respective gaining commands prior to marking aircraft.

4-9. USAF AIRCRAFT SUPPLIED UNDER MAP. All USAF aircraft that are to be reconditioned or rehabilitated for the Military Assistance Program (MAP) will be protected from corrosion by painting with standard Air Force material prior to delivery.

a. When a recipient country accepts delivery of Grant Aid aircraft in the CONUS and arranges for ferrying the aircraft with its own crew or agents, the title passes at that time to the recipient country. Therefore, all USAF insignia and markings will be removed prior to transfer. The recipient country will arrange to affix its insignia and markings on the aircraft prior to operation.

b. When Grant Aid aircraft are delivered by USAF pilots or by U.S. civilian or foreign national pilots under operational control of the U.S. Air Force, title will remain with the U.S. Government until the aircraft are delivered in the recipient country. Therefore, upon departure from the CONUS the aircraft will display temporarily installed USAF markings and will be cleared as USAF military aircraft. Temporary paint, Specification MIL-P-6884, shall be used for these markings. The temporary paint can be readily removed with naphtha without harming the permanent exterior finish.

c. It is the responsibility of the Chief of the Air Force Section of the MAAG, or appropriate military mission, to assure that USA insignia and markings are promptly removed upon arrival of the aircraft in the recipient country. In cases where the recipient country does not have the capability to install its insignia and markings, the Chief of the Air Force Section of the MAAG will make arrangements with the appropriate AFLC agency to have this done during aircraft deprocessing.

d. Aircraft to be delivered in crates or as deck loads on carriers shall have all USAF insignia and markings removed prior to processing for shipment.

4-10. AIRCRAFT PROPELLER MARKINGS. All Air Force aircraft propeller blade tips will normally be painted yellow. Measured from the tip of the blade toward the propeller hub, the width of the painted tip stripe will be four inches for propellers less than 15 feet in diameter. The blade tip stripe for propellers with diameters of 15 feet or larger will be six inches. Luster-less lacquer, Specification MIL-L-19538, orange-yellow, color number 33538, will be used for this application. The only authorized exceptions to the above specified provisions are contained in the following paragraphs.

a. Propeller tips may be marked with a yellow light-reflective liquid, aerosol spray type, when it is necessary to define the path of the propeller track in the dark.

b. Aircraft whose primary mission is the transportation of VIPs are authorized to have red, white, and blue propeller tips. Approval authority for designating these aircraft is limited to major commands and will not be delegated to any lower level of command. Indiscriminate approval of these markings will defeat the intent of this directive and therefore will not be condoned. The occasional use of aircraft to transport VIPs is not sufficient justification for the multi-colored propeller tips.

(1) Red, white, and blue propeller tips are authorized for the following aircraft:

(a) Air Attache.

(b) Military Assistance Advisory Group (MAAG).

(c) USAF Missions.

(d) 89th Military Airlift Wing, MAC.

(2) When authorized, the red, white, and blue stripes will be painted in that order on each blade, from the blade tip toward the hub.

(a) For aircraft propellers less than 15 feet in diameter, each stripe will be one and one-half inches wide.

(b) For aircraft propellers 15 feet or more in diameter, each stripe will be two inches wide.

NOTE

Propellers shall be checked for balance after complete finishing and required markings have been applied. Minor touchup is authorized between overhaul periods. However, care shall be taken to insure that a proportionate quantity of paint is applied on each blade.

4-11. HELICOPTER ROTOR BLADE MARKINGS. Classification numbers shall be stenciled on the main rotor blades of all helicopters by facilities authorized to balance or alter the blades. Three numbers, in decimal form, shall be utilized; the first shall be the weight of the blade in pounds; the second number shall reflect the distance in inches from the center of rotation to the center of gravity of the blade; the third number shall be the distance in inches from the leading edge of the blade to the center of gravity of the blade chord-wise.

EXAMPLE: "57.2-75.5-5.2" indicates that the blade has a weight of 57.2 pounds, with the center of gravity 75.5 inches from the center of rotation, and the chord-wise center of gravity is 5.2 inches from the lead edge of the blade. Stenciling, approximately 3/4 inch in height, shall be accomplished with a paint or dope which contrasts well with the color of the blade. The preceding information is to be stenciled on the flat surface of the ground side of each blade at the inboard or butt end of the main rotor blade.

NOTE

The color bands installed by the contractor on the tip of the main rotor blades shall be maintained along with matching colors on the housing. Different colors are required on the blades for tracking as well as matching purposes.

4-12. TAIL ROTOR BLADE MARKING. To promote ground safety, all helicopter tail rotor blades, except Sikorsky blades utilizing "B" and "B" bonding or having vinyl plastic tape installed, shall be marked as follows:

a. Prime surface with one light coat of lacquer primer, Specification MIL-P-7962.

b. Apply a six-inch band of red lacquer, Specification MIL-L-19538, color number 31136, to the tail rotor tip followed by a six-inch band of insignia white lacquer, Specification MIL-L-19538, color number 37875, and another six-inch band of red lacquer.

c. Following the second band of red lacquer, Specification MIL-L-19538, color number 31136, apply a band of black lacquer, Specification MIL-L-19538, color number 37038, to within six inches of the hub.

d. Paint the remaining six inches of the tail rotor blade with red lacquer, Specification MIL-L-19538, color number 31136.

NOTE

After application of these markings to the tail rotor blades of UH-1 helicopters, the use of a Strobex balancer will be used to rebalance blades.

NOTE

Identifying color bands painted on the tail rotor blade housing by the contractor shall be maintained and an identifying dot, approximately 1/2 inch in diameter, of the same color as appears on the housing shall be painted on the butt end of the blade for matching purposes.

4-13. INSTALLATION OF PLACARDS IN AIRCRAFT. Accomplish installation of aircraft cockpit placards required by interim technical orders by coating the back of the placard with a clear lacquer, varnish, or similar substance. Apply an additional coat of clear lacquer, varnish, or similar substance over the front of the placard.

4-14. IDENTIFICATION MARKINGS FOR JETTISONABLE AIRCRAFT COMPONENTS. Color of the enamel or lacquer used to stencil numbers and letters on jettisonable aircraft components will be dependent upon the color that provides the greatest contrast with the surrounding area and in accordance with Section II. The following components require identification:

a. Canopies. Jettisonable aircraft canopies shall have the aircraft radio call number stenciled on the outside or inside of the canopy frame on the left hand side six inches from the forward end, using one-inch high numbers provided sufficient space is available. If sufficient space is not available to accommodate one-inch high numbers, they will be as large as space permits.

b. Ejection Seats. All aircraft equipped with ejection seats shall have the aircraft radio call number stenciled on the front side of the seat back near the top edge, or on the left side near the top edge. Whenever aircraft are equipped with more than one seat, each shall be further identified according to that used by the respective crew members, i.e. PILOT, CO-PILOT, EWO, NAV, RAD-NAV, and GUNNER. These titles shall be applied directly below the radio call number. All the above listed markings shall be applied utilizing one-inch high numbers and letters. Position markings so as to avoid contact with parachute gear.

c. Jettisonable Components. Where jettisonable components such as wing and pylon tanks are interchangeable and are frequently removed and installed, and create a problem of stockpiling components for specific aircraft, the base supply account number as contained in USAF Supply Manual 67-1 will be applied to the component. The number will be stenciled on both sides and as near the center as possible using one-inch high numbers. This does not apply to jettisonable seats, canopies, or components that are not subject to frequent changes.

4-15. MARKING OF EMERGENCY LIGHTING (FLASHLIGHT) - CARGO AND TRANSPORT TYPE AIRCRAFT.

a. Cargo and transport type aircraft which have flashlights located adjacent to each natural or emergency exit as an emergency lighting system will have a band of phosphorescent paint, Federal Specification TT-P-54, approximately 1/2 inch wide applied around the base of the flashlight mounting. This will provide a rectangular frame outlining the light. The paint may be applied to the mounting flanges along the sides of the light holder if the installation is such that the paint cannot be applied to the surface on which the light mounting is installed.

b. Allow the phosphorescent paint to dry approximately eight hours, then apply a protective coat of varnish, Federal Specification TT-V-109, over it. This will lengthen the useful life of the paint.

4-16. MARKING FOR WALKWAYS AND HONEYCOMB PANELS.

a. Walkways and Steps. In cases where they do not contrast in color with adjacent areas, walkway areas shall be bounded by a camouflage black line for a light background or a camouflage white line for a dark background, 1/2 inch wide, and marked with the word "WALKWAY" at sufficiently frequent intervals to indicate the walkway area. Steps shall be suitably indicated at all points on the aircraft.

b. Honeycomb Panels on Airplanes. Honeycomb panels (thin skin) for wing upper surfaces shall be distinctly marked by a 1-1/2-inch wide stripe of hash marks; each hash mark shall be two inches long, measured along the stripe with two inches between marks. The marks shall slope 45 degrees. The marks shall be painted orange-yellow, color number 13538, using material that conforms to that used on adjacent areas.

4-17. MARKINGS FOR DRONES. Drones are any remotely controlled, recoverable, pilotless aircraft developed or modified to perform the mission of a target or weapon system. Drones will be marked and painted as follows:

a. Target Drones. Target drones for weapons evaluation, crew training, etc., shall be painted International Orange, color number 12197, with Specification MIL-L-19537 material.

NOTE

Normally, weapons systems that have been modified into drones will not be painted.

b. _Weapons System Drones._ Weapons system drones/ RPVs may be developed, tested, and deployed painted in the color scheme required for mission accomplishment. The paint schemes for these drones shall be approved for the intended purpose(s) as directed by AFR 66-34 and the specific technical orders applicable to the drones. Standard approved specification (military or Federal) finish materials in the color(s) required will be used to paint the exterior(s) of these drones.

NOTE

All numerals, letters, and markings, except the National Star Insignia applied on International Orange shall be black lacquer, Specification MIL-L-19537, color number 17038 (see Appendix A).

4-18. MARKINGS FOR SEARCH AND RESCUE AIRCRAFT. Aircraft engaged in search and rescue operations shall have markings applied as indicated in the following paragraphs using Specification MIL-C-83286.

a. _Wing Tips._ Upper and lower surfaces of both wing tips shall be painted orange-yellow, color number 13538, from the wing tip inboard a distance equal to 7% of the wing span (float excluded). A black border six inches wide shall be added inboard, using color number 17038.

b. _Vertical Stabilizer and Rudder._ Using vertical block type white letters, color number 17875, the word "RESCUE" shall be applied on a blue background, color number 15044, to both sides of the vertical stabilizer and rudder approximately spaced between the radio call numbers and the top of the vertical stabilizer. The letters will be a minimum of 12 inches in height. If larger lettering is used, the background should be increased proportionally. A three-inch wide orange-yellow band, color number 13538, shall be applied at the top and bottom of the blue background.

4-19. AIRCRAFT CONSPICUITY AND ARCTIC MARKINGS. Conspicuity and Arctic markings are of the same color and configuration for each aircraft and are as illustrated in Appendix B of this technical order.

a. _Conspicuity Markings._ Conspicuity markings may be used under special conditions on non-camouflaged aircraft and are intended to enhance air-to-air visual detection for safety purposes. Conspicuity markings will not normally be applied to Air Force aircraft except for those specifically authorized by this technical order as approved by HQ USAF/LGYY for specific aircraft engaged in special operations.

(1) Aircraft authorized conspicuity markings. The

following aircraft shall be required to have conspicuity markings applied:

(a) Aircraft used primarily as target aircraft.

(b) AFSC aircraft specifically designated by the major command headquarters, due to peculiar requirements of research and development programs. Included may be director and drone aircraft.

(c) AFCC flight inspection aircraft.

1 To enhance air-to-air low-level visual detection of aircraft performing airborne flight inspection of traffic control facilities, C-140 and T-39 aircraft shall be painted the standard Air Force gray, color number 16473, and white, color 17875, with conspicuity markings as specified in Appendix C - Special Purpose Aircraft Markings.

2 Special conspicuity markings are authorized only when 75% or more of the mission flying hours are utilized in enroute/on facility time.

b. _Arctic Markings._ The use of Arctic markings is intended to facilitate the location of aircraft accidentally downed in regions covered by ice or snow. Arctic markings will be applied to aircraft assigned for operation in the Arctic region during the period from 15 October through 15 April or for at least a six-month period in Antarctica. In North America, for purposes of this technical order, the Arctic region is that territory north of the 50th parallel.

(1) Arctic Marking Exemptions. Aircraft in the following categories are exempt from compliance with Arctic marking requirements:

(a) Air Attache assigned aircraft.

(b) Aircraft scheduled for short periods of duty less than 180 days in designated Arctic/Antarctic areas.

(c) Active strike force and combat support aircraft assigned offensive missions into or over Arctic/Antarctic areas for less than 180 days.

(d) All camouflaged USAF aircraft.

c. _Material Requirements for Conspicuity and Arctic Markings._ The material requirements for Arctic and/or conspicuity markings shall be compatible with the materials over which they are applied. Normally, this will be Specification MIL-C-83286, International Orange, color number 12197. Refer to TO 1-1-8 for application instructions.

d. _Change in Aircraft Mission Assignments._ In the event mission requirements change and conspicuity/

arctic markings are not needed, or if such markings are detrimental to the safe accomplishment of the mission, the painted or film markings will be removed. When time permits the markings will be stripped from the aircraft surfaces. When emergency conditions dictate the need, the markings will be over-painted.

4-20. ESTABLISHING NEW REQUIREMENTS FOR INSIGNIA AND MARKINGS. Requests for approval of other insignia and markings proposed for in-service aircraft not included in this technical order will be submitted to Warner Robins ALC/MMTRDC. Request for approval of new or additional insignia or markings must contain full justification and be accompanied by two sets of exterior surface drawings showing proposed marking locations on the aircraft, by applicable structural station number, water line reference points, dimensions, and color scheme. Aircraft markings which reflect mission activity, crew accomplishments, and crew esprit de corps allowed at the descretion and final approval of the senior logistics manager in each MAJCOM.[13]

----

13. [This last sentence reflects an important policy reversal, implemented with Change 29 on 15 August 1989. Previously, the last sentence read, "Aircraft markings which reflect mission activity, crew accomplishments, or which are for enhancement of crew esprit de corps, are prohibited by Hq USAF."]

SECTION V

STANDARD MARKINGS, FINISHES, AND INSIGNIA

FOR CAMOUFLAGED USAF AIRCRAFT

5-1. PURPOSE OF CAMOUFLAGE. Camouflage is used for purposes of deception, to conceal materiel from undesired observation, or to confuse and mislead observers as to identity, extent, number, etc. Pattern camouflage is applied to an aircraft to lessen probability of detection visually or photographically, in flight or on the ground. Pattern camouflaging is based on optical principles that dictate certain non-reflective colors, color configurations, and color proportions. Arbitrary applications of markings and color schemes other than those prescribed herein will defeat the purpose of camouflage and are not condoned. TO 1-1-8 provides instructions for surface preparation and application of coating materials for camouflaging aircraft.

5-2. CAMOUFLAGE AUTHORITY.

a. Authority to camouflage aircraft will be granted only by Headquarters USAF. Major commands will forward requests to camouflage aircraft to Headquarters USAF, LEYY, Hq USAF/XOOT, and Hq USAF/RDPN.

b. The management of Headquarters USAF approved aircraft camouflage programs resides at WR-ALC. All matters dealing with the adequacy of approved aircraft camouflage color schemes, effectiveness, techniques, or principles shall be forwarded to WR-ALC/MMTRDC for necessary action. Drawings and dimensions must accompany color scheme change requests.

c. The application or removal of aircraft camouflage coatings under emergency conditions, whereby the need for the required action is apparent, may be directed by the local commander. However, at the earliest opportunity, WR-ALC, Hq USAF/LEYY and Hq USAF/XOOT will be informed of the action taken and reason therefore.

5-3. AIRCRAFT CAMOUFLAGE MATERIALS. The standard materials for the camouflage coating system and insignia/marking application is aliphatic polyurethane camouflage (lusterless) Specification MIL-C-83286. Decals may be used in lieu of paint for insignia and markings provided that they are made of a non-reflective decal material (see Paragraph 3-3). Decals shall not be used with "gunship quality" schemes.

5-4. CAMOUFLAGE PATTERNS. Approved weapon system/camouflage pattern combinations are illustrated in Appendix D.

a. Aircraft Surfaces. The camouflage patterns shall be applied in accordance with the specific aircraft illustrations. The illustrations are intended as guides. Minor variations in pattern are acceptable; however, care should be taken that proportion and balance of the different colors are approximately the same as the illustrations. Boundaries between colors shall be irregular as illustrated and fade into each other. Avoid sharp lines between colors.

b. Bottom Surfaces. Most camouflaged aircraft use a singular color on the underside of the fuselage, wings, horizontal stabilizer, and control surfaces as designed for the particular weapon system. The bottom color shall be brought up the sides of the fuselage to give the approximate side view appearance in accordance with the application illustration. The line between the underbelly color and the upper surface pattern shall be an irregular, indistinct, countershaded area. A sharp line and any regular repeating pattern such as a scallop will raise the risk of detection and compromise the overall camouflage effect. On low wing aircraft, the bottom color on the fuselage is brought into the wing root to meet the bottom color under the wing.

c. External Components. Engine nacelles, external tanks, pods, and other mounted equipment shall be camouflage-painted to agree with the aircraft scheme. Unless otherwise specified, the lower third of the surface shall be the same as the bottom color for the aircraft and the upper surfaces shall be pattern-painted or painted a designated solid color as approved for the weapon system. With appropriate approvals, the entire surface of this equipment and pylons may be all painted one uniform color to improve component interchangeability on different aircraft or on different positions on the same aircraft. The extent to which this can be accomplished and the choice of color shall be in accordance with the system or item technical order when it involves a surface which is not covered or illustrated in this general manual.

d. Radomes, Antennae, and Antenna Covers. Antennae shall be treated in accordance with the Item or System Manager. Radomes and antenna covers should be over-sprayed with a light coat of camouflage finish to make the camouflage effort complete unless the System Manager determines that the paint deters operational capabilities and prohibits its use.

e. Walkways. Walkway borders shall be applied to the upper surfaces of camouflaged aircraft in black, color number 37038.

f. Gunship Quality Paint Systems. The European I camouflage scheme and certain other weapon system/camouflage scheme combinations require the use of "gunship quality" paint. Gunship quality paint is special formulation polyurethane paint that is available in several camouflage color numbers. It meets physical requirements of Specification MIL-C-83286, and certain additional requirements for gloss and sheen not presently standard under Specification MIL-C-83286. At the present time, this is a controlled-source paint. The authorized sources are DeSoto, Inc, Des Plaines, Illinois, and Berkeley, California, and Deft Chemical Coating, Irvine, California. Always be certain that the paint vendor or immediate supply activity knows when you require gunship quality. Standard camouflage in the same color numbers does not provide the required performance.

5-5. INSIGNIA AND MARKINGS. The following exceptions to standard USAF insignia and markings as listed in Section III are applicable to USAF camouflaged aircraft:

a. "U.S. AIR FORCE" Markings. The "U.S. AIR FORCE" marking on the forward fuselage is not required.

b. National Star Insignia. The National Star Insignia shall be applied to the top of the left wing, the bottom of the right wing, and on both sides of the fuselage in a miniaturized configuration. The standard design is illustrated in Figure A-1.

c. USAF and Radio Call Number Marking. The "USAF" marking shall not be applied to the wings; but, shall be added immediately before the radio call number on the vertical fin if space is available. Otherwise, place directly above the radio call number. The radio call number and "USAF" marking shall be of a miniaturized configuration, unless the aircraft has been approved for distinctive unit aircraft markings as outlined in Paragraph 5-9.

d. Deleted.

e. Location and Size of Miniaturized Insignia and Markings.

MARKING	LOCATION	SIZE
National Star Insignia	Top of left wing, bottom of right wing, and both sides of fuselage on winged aircraft	15 inches (except 60 inches on upper wing and 18 inches on fuselage, B-52 aircraft).
Radio Call Number	Both sides vertical stabilizer or tail boom (radio call numbers will be constructed IAW Paragraph 3-2. See Paragraph 5-9 and Appendix D for distinctive unit markings.)	6 inches high (except 12 inches high on B-52 aircraft).
Radio Call Number	At Air Refueling receptacle	4 inches high.
"USAF"	Immediately before radio call number, if space available. If not, directly over radio call [tail] number.	6 inches high (except 60 inches on upper wing B-52 aircraft).

NOTE

To assist in the identification of aircraft during ground handling, it is permitted to apply the last three numerals of the aircraft serial number to the lower forward portion of the fuselage side in six-inch letters.

f. Colors. Colors of insignia and markings shall be as follows:

(1) Gunship-quality camouflage shall use only gunship-quality contrasting colors for all exterior insignia and markings. Waiver or deviation will be considered only when the requirement for gunship quality is no longer essential.

(2) Standard camouflage exterior insignia and markings shall be subdued black, color number 37038, except those special markings covered in Paragraphs (a), (b), and (c).

(a) Required safety precautionary markings shall be red, color number 31136.

(b) External markings identifying escape hatches, doors, exits, and emergency entry or exits shall be orange-yellow, color number 33538. (See Paragraphs 6-15 through 6-17 which apply to standard camouflaged and uncamouflaged aircraft.)

(c) Camouflage schemes in the SEA configuration use white markings on black backgrounds except with gunship quality which shall use contrasting gunship quality color.

5-6. INSTRUCTIONAL MARKINGS. Instructional type markings for servicing, ground handling, etc., shall be kept to the minimum required by the System Manager to be consistent with safety, performance, and maintenance of the aircraft.

5-7. SQUADRON AND ORGANIZATIONAL MARK-INGS. Squadron and organizational markings may be used on camouflaged aircraft. Use the same criteria for the development of size as is used on non-camouflaged aircraft. The width of the horizontal stripes applied to the upper extremity of the vertical stabilizers will be six inches.

5-8. ARMAMENT LOADS PLACARD. Placards indicating armament loads shall be appropriately applied on camouflaged aircraft in accordance with SM instructions. (See Paragraph 6-18, Figures E-8 and E-10.)

5-9. DISTINCTIVE UNIT AIRCRAFT IDENTIFI-CATION MARKINGS. Distinctive unit aircraft markings may be applied to vertical fins of camouflaged combat support aircraft to allow aircrews to readily identify aircraft to their own unit or to other friendly units. The master coding system to be utilized is USAF wide to avoid code duplication among units. TAC has been designated by HQ USAF as the Air Force single manager for the assignment of unit aircraft identification markings.

a. Essentially, the codes consist of: (1) two alphabetic letters, (2) two numerical digits, or (3) an alphabetic letter and a numerical digit. Using major commands may authorize the use of these identification markings but shall receive the approved coding to be used from Headquarters TAC. When the codes are no longer required, the respective major command shall appropriately notify TAC.

NOTE

In no instance will these unit identification codes be installed or removed without the expressed knowledge and approval of TAC. Similarly, only TAC may authorize changes in identification code assignments.

b. Instructions for the design, dimensions, and location of the distinctive unit aircraft identification codes are contained in Appendix D.

c. Aircraft tail numbers (identified as serial number in applicable part of Appendix D) will consist of the first two and last three digits of the original serial number. When duplicate last three digits exist among aircraft with the same distinctive unit aircraft identification designator, the last four digits of the aircraft serial number shall be used. This number serves as the radio call number for aircraft with distinctive unit markings.

5-10. SPECIAL OPERATING FORCE (SOF) AIRCRAFT. The gray paint finish (aliphatic polyurethane Specification MIL-C-83286, color number 16473) with standard Air Force markings is the normal exterior paint configuration for SOF aircraft. However, inasmuch as the SOF aircraft are subject to various mission assignments, in different geographical locations and under varying circumstances, the specific mission will dictate the aircraft exterior configuration required for the affected aircraft. In all instances, changes in paint configurations of these aircraft will be accomplished only as a result of firm mission requirements and not for reasons of esthetics or personal preference.

a. Some major reasons which may require changes in the exterior paint configuration of SOF aircraft are:

(1) Need for ground-to-air or air-to-air camouflage or conspicuity.

(2) Need for air-to-ground or ground-to-ground camouflage or conspicuity.

(3) National image or national interest.

(4) Discrete aircraft employment.

b. Normally, request for approval of proposed changes to exterior paint configurations for SOF aircraft not engaged in combat operations shall be forwarded by the major command to Hq USAF/LEYY and Hq USAF/XOOT.

c. Whenever conditions warrant, the major command may authorize the application of needed exterior paint configurations for SOF aircraft engaged in combat operations without prior approval or higher authority. Whenever possible, Air Force standard materials will be used. All changes to SOF aircraft configurations shall be promptly reported to WR-ALC/MMTRDC and to Hq USAF/LEYY and Hq USAF/XOOT accompanied by appropriate descriptive 8"x10" photograph and drawings on 8"x10" paper, reasons for the changes, and results achieved.

5-11. NATO MARKINGS CODE NUMBERS. The application of North Atlantic Treaty Organization (NATO) code numbers cited in TO 42B1-1-15 shall supplement the applicable service points prescribed in Appendix E. The codes will be applied immediately adjacent to the symbol as considered most practical. NATO code numbers may be omitted when not reflected in TO 42B1-1-15 or may be omitted on training type aircraft and other aircraft not subject to being serviced at overseas locations.

NOTE

Certain provisions of this section are subject to internal standardization agreements (see Air Standardization Coordinating Committee Air Standard 11/1D and NATO, STANAG 3109) and shall not be changed except under emergency conditions without prior coordination with the Air Standardization Coordinating Committee (ASCC). All requests or recommendations for changes in existing markings or supplemental markings will be submitted to WR-ALC/MMTRDC, for appropriate action.

5-12. Deleted.

5-13. Deleted.

SECTION VI

SERVICING, GROUND HANDLING, EMERGENCY, AND

HAZARD WARNING MARKINGS, (NON-CAMOUFLAGED)

AIRCRAFT

6-1. GENERAL. The requirement for and location of these markings will vary with the aircraft configuration. Printed information required in connection with ground handling or servicing symbols shall be painted in black or white depending on the background. Lettering sizes shall be in accordance with instructions in Appendix E. Capital letters and Arabic numerals shall be used.

a. Identification Symbols. Symbols for the identification of servicing points, ground handling locations, emergency use, and hazard warning shall be applied to required locations on all USAF aircraft to provide the following:

(1) Rapid identification of each required servicing point.

(2) Identification of the type of ground servicing required.

(3) Hazard warning or safety precautions which will prevent injury to personnel or damage to aircraft equipment.

(4) Rapid entry or exit from vehicle under emergency conditions.

b. Illustrations. Illustrations of the prescribed symbols to be used are contained in Appendix E. This technical order may be applied using appropriate paint or decalcomania. Symbol size shall be approximately four inches in the longest dimension; however, smaller-sized symbols may be used if required by the item or area to be marked. Color requirement for symbols shall be as follows:

(1) Filling points symbols shall be colored black or white according to the background.

(2) Ground handling point symbols shall be colored orange-yellow, color number 13538, and have a black or white outline according to the background.

(3) Safety or hazard warning symbols shall be colored red and have a black or white outline according to the background.

(4) Emergency exit or entry location markings will be colored orange-yellow, color number 13538. Black markings, color number 17038, will be used on yellow surfaces.

c. Locations. The location of each marking shall be dependent upon the existing available space. They may be situated on the equipment concerned, directly below, adjacent to, or on applicable access panels. In event the service point or marking is concealed, arrows may be used to point out the location of the service point or markings. The arrow should bear a brief identification of the purpose for which it is applied, the applicable service point identification or precautionary warning marking.

6-2. NATO MARKING CODE NUMBERS. The application of North Atlantic Treaty Organization (NATO) code numbers cited in TO 42B1-1-15 shall supplement the applicable service points prescribed in Appendix E. The codes shall be applied immediately adjacent to the symbol.

a. The application of NATO code numbers will be waived when it is not reflected in TO 42B1-1-15 or may be omitted on training type aircraft and other aircraft not subject to being serviced at overseas locations.

b. Certain provisions of this section are subject to international standardization agreements (see Air Standardization Coordinating Committee Air Standard 11/1D and NATO STANAG 3109) and shall not be changed except under emergency conditions without prior coordination with the Air Standardization Coordinating Committee (ASCC). All requests or recommendations for changes in existing markings or supplemental markings shall be submitted to WR-ALC/LKJTC for appropriate action.

6-3. HYDRAULIC SYSTEMS AND LANDING GEAR/ STRUTS. Servicing instructions for hydraulic systems, landing gear, and shock struts shall be provided on metal instruction plates or stenciled in a permanent and legible manner adjacent to charging points and test connections. (See applicable technical order.)

6-4. AIRCRAFT GROUNDING POINTS. All grounding points on all Air Force aircraft will be marked with part number MS27606, Decalcomania, Ground Here, International Symbol (see Figure E-3). Decals will be requisitioned from 2852d ABGp/DAPR,

McClellan AFB, California 95652, on AF Form 124A Publications/Forms Requisition.

6-5. STORAGE BATTERIES. The notation "BATTERY LOCATION _____" with exact battery location given shall be placed on the left side of the fuselage.

a. The fore and aft location of the marking will be approximately in line with the trailing edge of the wing and at a point two or three feet off the ground with the aircraft in the wheels-up position and resting on the ground, or in case of aircraft having fixed landing gears, with the landing gear washed out.

b. In the event of interference with windows, enclosures, etc., the marking shall placed as near the aforementioned location as is practicable.

c. In addition to the above markings, all battery locations on the interior of the aircraft will have the word "BATTERY" or "BATTERIES," as the case may be, permanently and conspicuously affixed to the battery casing or compartment. The marking shall be in one-inch high letters. The color will be red, number 11136.

d. Aircraft having exterior access to the batteries will have the word "BATTERY," "BATTERIES," or "BATTERY ACCESS" stenciled on the access door in one-inch high letters. The color for the exterior markings will be red, color number 11136 for non-camouflaged aircraft.

6-6. EJECTION SEATS. A red equilateral triangle with sides up to nine inches long, with the apex pointing downward shall be applied on each side of the fuselage adjacent to the explosive device. (See Appendix E.)

6-7. IDENTIFICATION OF BALLISTIC HOSE OR TUBING ASSEMBLIES. Ballistic hose or tubing assemblies leading to the ejection seat catapults shall be marked for ground rescue purposes. The marking on the hose or tubing shall be a band approximately eight inches long of orange-yellow enamel, Type 1, color number 13538, conforming to Specification TT-E-489. The area selected shall be easily visible, readily accessible, and as close as possible to the catapult.

6-8. CANOPY REMOVERS. Aircraft containing an explosive jettisonable canopy system shall be marked "WARNING - THIS AIRCRAFT CONTAINS A CANOPY REMOVER CONTAINING AN EXPLOSIVE CHARGE" and such other pertinent notations as "SEE TO _____ FOR COMPLETE INSTRUCTIONS."

6-9. MARKING FOR ELECTRICAL CONNECTIONS. The following caution note shall be placed at points where it is necessary to break electrical connections when folding back or removing wings:

CAUTION

DISCONNECT ELECTRICAL WIRING BEFORE

REMOVING WINGS

6-10. MARKINGS FOR ENGINE REMOVAL. To facilitate engine removal, all points of disconnect will be painted with International Orange paint, color number 12197, for identity.

6-11. MARKINGS FOR TANKS AND TANK FILLER AREAS.

a. Aircraft tanks, such as fuel, water/alcohol, engine oil, hydraulic fluid, deicing fluid, etc., shall have notations stenciled thereon, indicating tank capacity, type of liquid, and liquid level restrictions.

b. Fuel filler caps shall be painted red, color number 11136. Where flush type pressure caps, MS29525, are installed, three radial black lines (3/8 inch wide by 1 inch long typical), color number 38078, shall be located to form an extension to the lines on the cap when the cap is in the locked postion. A red band, color number 11136, one inch wide, around and two inches away from a fuel filler cap or cover door is optional.

c. Data, such as water-alcohol mixture or type and grade of other servicing fluids, shall be stenciled near the applicable filler cap in 1/2-inch high letters.

d. The following legend will be stenciled near fuel tank filler caps: "USE _____ OCTANE FUEL" or "USE GRADE _____ FUEL," as applicable.

6-12. MARKING FOR ENGINE COMPARTMENT FIRE ACCESS PANEL. The fire access panel or doors in the engine compartments shall have red, color number 11136, border and identifying text as illustrated in Appendix E, Figure E-4.

6-13. HELICOPTER TAIL ROTOR WARNING SIGN. A warning sign shall be painted on both sides of the tail booms of all helicopters employing vertical tail rotors. A typical example of the recommended warning is shown in Appendix E, and minor variations make it adaptable to all types of helicopters. The letters shall be approximately two inches high with warning arrow of appropriate size as indicated in reference Figure E-5.

6-14. PROPELLER WARNING STRIPES AND SIGNS.

a. Exterior. Mark that area of the fuselage which is in the plane of the propeller path with a red stripe three inches wide extending completely around the fuselage, whenever it does not interfere with standard USAF markings, insignia, or solar-resistant finishes. (See Appendix E, Figure E-10.)

NOTE

The propeller warning stripe shall not extend through standard USAF markings or insignia.

Maintain a space of three inches between the ends of the propeller warning stripe and any standard USAF marking or insignia. The word "PROPELLER" reading vertically from top to bottom shall be superimposed on this stripe in white, color number 17875, two-inch-high letters placed at sufficiently frequent intervals to indicate the dangerous area. The word "DANGER" shall be applied perpendicular to the word "PROPELLER" on each side of the warning stripe, with an arrow pointing from the word "DANGER" toward the stripe. Letters in the word "DANGER" shall be two inches high and the arrows shall be four inches long. The word "DANGER" and the arrows shall be red, color number 31136. The propeller warning stripe for those aircraft that have been painted Jet Black shall be white, color number 17875. The word "PROPELLER" superimposed thereon shall be red, color number 31136; the word "DANGER" and the arrows shall be white, color number 17875.

NOTE

On aircraft having engines staggered on the wing, propeller warning stripe shall also be placed on the cowling of the next inboard engine to mark the plane of rotation of the propeller disc.

b. <u>Interior.</u> An Insignia Red warning stripe, three inches wide, shall be marked inside the fuselage on both sides of bomb-bays, or other openings within six feet of either side of the propeller disc to warn personnel of the proximity of propellers, if such openings can be used as exits from the aircraft and if there is danger of personnel walking into propellers after leaving the openings. Stripes shall extend from the center of the fuselage or the top of the opening, whichever is higher, to the lowest extremity of the opening. The word "PROPELLER," reading vertically from top to bottom, shall be superimposed on the stripes in white, color number 17875, letters two inches high, to indicate dangerous area. The word "DANGER" in red, color number 31136, shall be applied perpendicular to and centered with respect to the word "PROPELLER" on each side of the stripe with a red, color number 31136, arrow pointing toward the stripe. Letters shall be two inches high and arrows four inches long. (See Appendix E, Figure E-10.)

6-15. REMOVABLE ESCAPE PANELS.

a. <u>Internal Markings.</u> Markings for identification of escape hatches, doors, and exits on the interior of aircraft shall be painted orange-yellow, color number 13538. Use black, color number 17038, on yellow surfaces. Materials for identification markings shall conform to Specification TT-E-489 or MIL-L-19537. Retroflective material conforming to Specification L-S-300 may be used for these markings to facilitate identification in the dark.

(1) Paint an intermittent orange-yellow band to mark the periphery of the personnel escape exit. The segments of the band will have a minimum width of one inch and a maximum length of two inches, divided equally, if possible and practicable, between the door mounting and the escape door itself. Where the lining will cover the identification marking band on the inside of the aircraft, continue the marking onto the lining.

(2) The words "EMERGENCY EXIT," in orange-yellow, shall be painted or stenciled on the escape hatch, door, or exit or any covering thereof in the most readily visible location. Letters will preferably be two inches high and shall not be less than one inch wide.

(3) Paint handles, releases, catches, and knobs for inside hatches and exit doors orange-yellow. Where lettering or marking areas are covered by lining (including sound proofing), the lining shall also be appropriately marked. Suitable descriptive wording, readily visible, shall be painted or stenciled on the door or structure of the aircraft, whichever is nearer the emergency release, to identify and explain its operation. This wording shall be at least 1/2 inch high and preferably one inch high. Use standard English terminology such as "PULL," "PUSH," "TURN," or "SLIDE."

(4) Exits which are adequate for air, ground, and ditching escape shall have the words "EMERGENCY EXIT" centered in the most visible location on the inside of the door or hatch.

(5) Exits which are not adequate for the above three methods of escape shall be marked "EMERGENCY EXIT" and for specific usage as follows: "GROUND USE ONLY," "GROUND AND DITCHING USE ONLY," ETC.

b. <u>External Markings.</u>

(1) Markings identifying escape hatches, doors, and exits on the outside of aircraft shall be orange-yellow, color number 13538; on yellow surface use black, color number 17038. If lacquer is used, it will conform to Specification MIL-L-19537; if polyurethane is used, it will conform to Specification MIL-C-83286. Retroflective material conforming to Specification L-S-300 may be

used for these markings to facilitate identification in the dark.

(2) Mark all external releases for operation of emergency exit panels "EXIT RELEASE" on the outside of the aircraft to facilitate quick identification. The wording that describes the operation of the exit release will be standard English terminology such as "PULL," "PUSH," "TURN," or "SLIDE." Letters shall be at least one inch high and preferably two inches high.

NOTE

Certain provisions of this section pertaining to emergency escape and entry markings are subject to international standardization agreements (see ASCC Air Standard 51/2A and NATO STANAG 3230) and shall not be changed except under emergency conditions without prior coordination with the Air Standardization Coordinating Committee. All requests for changes in existing markings or supplemental markings will be submitted to HQ WR-ALC/LKJTC

6-16. MARKINGS FOR FORCED EMERGENCY ENTRY OR EXIT.

a. Markings for aircraft emergency entry or exit shall normally be in orange-yellow, color number 13538. Use black, color number 17038, on orange-yellow backgrounds. Paint will conform to Specification MIL-C-83286. Retro-flective material conforming to Specification L-S-300 may be used for these markings to facilitate identification in the dark.

b. Secondary openings such as auxiliary exits, windows, and navigator's domes are usually smaller than primary openings, making entrance or exit more difficult. If the structure immediately surrounding secondary openings is free from heavy structural members such as bulkheads and main longitudinal members, and free from oxygen, fuel, and oil lines, and battery leads, it shall be marked with an orange-yellow broken band. Place band at the extreme boundary of the above described area both inside and outside of the fuselage. Segments of the broken band shall be 1/2 inch wide, one inch long, and approximately twelve inches apart. Where the band will be covered with soundproofing, the soundproofing (or lining) shall be marked also. "CUT HERE FOR EMERGENCY RESCUE" shall be printed or stenciled inside of, parallel with, and adjacent to the broken band identifying the area on the <u>outside</u> of the aircraft where forced entry can be made for rescue purposes. "CUT HERE FOR EMERGENCY EXIT" shall be painted on a similar location inside the aircraft. Letters shall be one inch high. If the area to receive the lettering is covered by

soundproofing (or lining), the letters shall also be stenciled on the soundproofing (or lining).

c. Visually inspect the aircraft for areas which may be cut through for rescue when entrance or exit cannot be made in any other manner. Visual inspection must be used because relocation and reinstallation of equipment and furnishings may have been made which would not be indicated on the installation drawing of the aircraft. These areas should be as close to normal stations of personnel as possible except that they shall not be placed where personal injury to occupants would probably result from forced entry. Paint or stencil corner markings on the inside and outside of the fuselage marking the limits of these areas. The horizontal and vertical bars of the corner markings shall be three inches long and one inch wide. "CUT HERE FOR EMERGENCY RESCUE" shall be painted or stenciled in the center of the four corner markings on the outside of the aircraft and "CUT HERE FOR EMERGENCY EXIT" shall be placed in a similar location inside the aircraft. Letters shall be one inch in height. Soundproofing, if installed, shall be painted or stenciled appropriately. These markings need not be placed on aircraft which are of such construction that openings could not be cut into them with safety.

CAUTION

Cutting of fuel, oil, hydraulic lines, oxygen lines, or electrical wiring under crash conditions may result in a fire or explosion, or increase the severity of an existing fire. These possibilities shall be taken into consideration when emergency escape areas are being chosen for identification markings.

6-17. SPECIAL MARKINGS FOR NORMAL/EMERGENCY EXTERNAL CANOPY RELEASE ACCESSES ON JET AIRCRAFT.

a. All normal and emergency external canopy release accesses on jet aircraft will be painted orange-yellow, color number 13538.

b. Canopies and hatches jettisoned by cartridge actuated devices shall be marked in accordance with examples portrayed in Appendix E.

6-18. ARMAMENT LOADS PLACARD. Placards may be applied either by painting or decal methods. Each System Manager is responsible to assure that standard armament placard locations are established for assigned aircraft, and that these requirements are published in this technical order. (See Appendix E, Figure E-9.)

a. <u>Paint Method.</u> If the painting method is desired, apply in accordance with dimensions and instructions in Figure E-8.

b. <u>Decal Method.</u> If the decal method is desired, apply in accordance with instructions contained in Figure E-9.

NOTE

Decals may be obtained from SM-ALC, PDO 2852d ABGp/DAPR, McClellan AFB, California 95652, on an Air Force Form 124A. Dash numbers (1) through (4) are applicable to standard Air Force camouflage patterns. Dash number (5) is applicable to standard non-camouflaged aircraft. Dash number (6) is applicable to special project, black bottom, camouflaged aircraft. It is important that the background color be the same as the area to which applied on camouflaged aircraft; therefore, selection of the correct dash number when ordering is required.

6-19. INSTRUMENT STATIC OPENING MARKINGS. Instrument static opening (except as noted below) shall not have any finish applied within a one-inch diameter circle around the opening.[14]

a. <u>F-4 Aircraft.</u> Static opening(s) on F-4 aircraft is on the radome which must be coated. However, the red 1/2-inch wide circular band shall be applied around the static opening(s) and the legend shall be applied adjacent to the opening.

b. Deleted.

---

14. [This paragraph originally included the sentences, "A red 1/2-inch wide circular band shall be applied around this area. The following legend shall also be applied adjacent to the marking INSTRUMENT STATIC OPENING - DO NOT COVER."]

SECTION VII

IDENTIFICATION OF TUBES, HOSE, AND PIPELINES

FOR AIRCRAFT

7-1. GENERAL. This section prescribes the means for identifying the function, content, and, if applicable, the hazard and direction of flow of pipe, hose and tube lines used in Air Force aircraft. The proper use of colors, words, symbols, tags, and painted bands to identify functions, contents, and hazards is specifically prescribed. Lines, as referred to herein, include any pipe, hose or tube used to convey liquids or gasses. Rigid conduit used to house electrical wires of cables are included. Fittings, valves, conduit outlets and accessories such as pipe covering and hose clamps are considered parts of a line. (Appendix F contains illustrations of pertinent codes and symbols to be used).

NOTE

International Standardization Agreement. Certain provisions of this section are subject to international standardization agreements and must not be changed except under emergency conditions without prior coordination with the Air Standardization Coordinating Committee (see ASCC Air Standard 17/3, STANAG 3104 and SEASTAG 3104). Therefore, all requests for changes in existing markings or supplemental markings will be submitted to Headquarters WR-ALC, Attn: MMTRDC.

NOTE

This section contains the identification requirements of MIL-STD-1247 as applicable to aircraft.

7-2. GENERAL CLASSIFICATION OF LINES.

a. Cold Lines - Lines in which the temperature of the flowing medium is below minus 60 degrees Fahrenheit.

b. Hot Lines - Lines on which the surface temperature ranges from 200 degrees to 325 degrees Fahrenheit.

c. Instrument Air - Air used on conjunction with pressure operated instruments.

d. Pneumatic - Air under pressure other than instrument air.

e. Compressed Gas - Any gaseous substance under pressure, other than air, not requiring other functional identification.

7-3. GENERAL MARKING OF LINES. Identify each line as to function, content, hazard and direction of flow, applicable.

a. Function - is identified by use of words, colors and symbols. Coded tapes will normally be used for airborne lines, except that small tags of some light-weight non-corrosive metal such as aluminum alloy, stamped with contents, pressure and direction of flow, may be used on airborne cold lines.

NOTE

Symbols and colors are not required on lines where identification is accomplished with aluminum alloy tag.

b. Content - is identified by use of lettering and symbols.

c. Hazard - is identified by use of lettering and symbols.

d. Direction of flow - is identified by arrow. Use two-headed arrow for reversible flow.

e. Pressure - is identified by numerals and lettering, indicating pounds per square inch (PSI).

7-4. METHOD FOR IDENTIFICATION OF LINES.

a. Tape. Use color coded tape conforming to Specification MIL-T-9906 for identifying function of all lines less than four inches in diameter including hot lines where line surface temperatures do not exceed 325 degrees Fahrenheit. Tapes may also be used in an oily environment provided adhesion can be maintained. Do not use tape in engine compartment where there is a possibility of tape being drawn into engine intake. Use Specification MS16837 tapes for further identification of lines. When applying tape to lines, the tape shall completely encircle the line. Thoroughly clean the portion of the line where the tape is to be applied. Place taped code on both ends of line. Insure that identification is visible in each compartment. Place identification tape immediately adjacent to all operating accessories such as valves, regulators, strainers, vents, etc.

NOTE

Cold lines may be identified by use of tape, provided adhesion can be maintained at cryogenic temperatures and can be read from point of operation.

b. Tags. Tags will not normally be used except for lines in an oily environment, hot lines exceeding 325 degrees Fahrenheit and cold lines. Tags will be of self locking design as illustrated in Appendix F. Fabricate tags from aluminum alloy. Stamp to show function and contents (pressure, direction of flow, primary hazard, as applicable). Color coding is not required on aluminum tags. Locate metal tags adjacent to operating accessories, making certain they will not interfere with the operation of the accessory.

c. Paint conforming to Specification TT-E-489 or MIL-C-83286 shall be used to identify lines in engine compartments where there is a possibility of tapes being drawn into engine intakes. Paint lines larger than four inches in diameter, except that cold lines, hot lines, and lines in an oily environment, shall conform to the following requirements.

(1) Lines will be color coded with paint in accordance with Appendix F. Painted code bands will be located adjacent to operating accessories, function with branch lines and where lines pass through bulkheads.

(2) Stencils are suitable for painting the letters to identify the specific function and contents (working pressure, primary hazard, and direction of flow arrow, as applicable). Geometric symbols are not required where identification is accomplished with paints. Use black lettering on white background.

(3) Size of painted lettering and arrow.

(a) Lines four to eight inches diameter - lettering height 1-1/4 inches.

(b) Lines eight to ten inches diameter - lettering height 2-1/2 inches.

(c) Lines over ten inches diameter - lettering height 3-1/2 inches.

(d) Width of arrow stem 1/8th maximum diameter of line. Total length of arrow will be equal to diameter of lines.

(4) Word Order. The words denoting function will appear first in the printed identification. The content description will appear immediately below the statement of function. Following below these, if applicable, will be the operating pressure, the painted arrow indicating direction of flow and the words denoting the hazard. Vertical spacing shall be such that all wording and flow symbols are evenly spaced from top to bottom of the viewing area.

7-5. ELECTRICAL CONDUITS. Identify wire carrying conduits with coded tape provided for electrical conduit. Add two additional markings: (1) Usage, i.e., power, control, communication, etc. (2) Maximum voltage and type normally encountered, i.e., "115V 60 cycle AC," "28 VDC," etc. Conduit carrying a number of different wires serving different purposes will be marked "ELECTRICAL CONDUIT" (including symbol of it on tapes) only. However, those conduits which constitute a hazard to operating personnel shall be marked to indicate the maximum voltage normally encountered.

7-6. FLEXIBLE CABLES. Whether metal or metal sheathed need not be identified.

7-7. AIR CONDITIONING DUCTS. Identify air conditioning ducts under 30 inches outside circumference with appropriate tape. Add tape indicating design temperature of flowing medium. Use paint (black lettering on white background) to identify larger than 30 inches outside circumference. Letter with 1-1/2-inch letters "AIR CONDITIONING" in two lines, followed by third line indicating temperature of flowing medium. The sign should be as large as possible, but not to exceed 12 x 12 inches.

APPENDIX A

STANDARD AIR FORCE AIRCRAFT MARKINGS

A-1. NATIONAL STAR INSIGNIA

a. <u>Dimensions.</u> (Figure A-1.) The dimensions of the insignia shall be determined by the diameter of the circumscribed circle which is standardized in multiples of five inches.

(1) The width of each end of the rectangle shall be 1/2 the radius of the circle; the length shall be equal to one radius (excluding border).

(2) The width of the Insignia-Red stripes, horizontally centered in each rectangle, shall equal 1/6 of the radius of the circle (excluding border).

(3) The width of the Insignia-Blue border shall equal 1/8 the radius of the circle (excluding border).

(4) Construction of the five-pointed star may be accomplished by marking off five equidistant points on the circumscribed circle and connecting each point to the non-adjacent points.

NOTE

The Insignia-Blue border and Insignia-Blue circle may be omitted when the National Star Insignia is applied on blue or black finishes.

CAUTION

Sharp, pointed, metal marking instruments (scribes) will not be used to lay out insignia and markings on USAF aircraft. Use only Aircraft Marking Pencil, Specification MIL-P-83953.

b. <u>National Star Insignia on Aircraft Wings.</u> Each insignia will be positioned at a point inboard from each wing tip equal to 1/3 the distance from the wing tip to the wing-fuselage mating point. The border of the insignia will be tangent to the movable control surface cut-out.

(1) The wing insignia may be moved in the minimum required distance to avoid structures which would alter the insignia pattern. However, symmetry will be maintained with the "USAF" marking on the opposite wing surface.

(2) Normally the wing insignia shall be positioned so that in normal flight attitude the top point of the star

points forward and a line through the center of the insignia and the top star point is parallel to the direction of flight.

(3) On swept wings or wings of variable-sweep aircraft, the National Star Insignia shall be positioned as illustrated in Figure A-2. The insignia or any part thereof shall not extend to movable flight control surfaces. The insignia shall be applied so that the line through the center and the top point is perpendicular to the constant 50% chord line of the wing.

(4) The National Star Insignia selected for the wing shall not exceed a maximum diameter of 60 inches nor have a minimum diameter of less than 20 inches (excluding border). The diameter of the circumscribed circle will be the standard size closest to, but not exceeding, 75% of the distance between the wing leading edge and the moveable surface cut-out at the point of application.

c. <u>National Star Insignia on Aircraft Fuselage.</u> The insignia may be moved forward or aft the minimum distance required to avoid transparent material or areas exposed to extreme heat or fluids which would scorch, deteriorate, or otherwise damage the insignia. The insignia may extend over doors and emergency exits, but the insignia shall not extend over window areas or other such openings which would change the design of the insignia.

NOTE

The insignia will be the standard size closest to, but not exceeding, 75% of the fuselage height at the point of application. The diameter of the blue circle will not exceed 50 inches nor be less than 15 inches (excluding border) unless otherwise indicated in the illustrated portion of this technical manual. Symmetry will be maintained when applying the insignia on each side of the fuselage.

d. <u>National Star Insignia on Helicopters.</u> The dimensions of the insignia shall be determined by the diameter of the blue circle. The diameter of the insignia will not exceed 50 inches nor be less than 15 inches. The selected insignia will be the standard size closest to, but not exceeding, 75% of the fuselage height or width at the point of application. Symmetry will be maintained when applying insignia on each side of the fuselage. The National Star Insignia will be applied on vertical surfaces so that in normal flight attitude the top point of the star points forward; on horizontal surfaces the top point of the star will point forward in the direction of flight.

A-2. "U.S. AIR FORCE" MARKING. (Figures A-3 and A-4.)

a. Letter width shall be equal to 2/3 of the letter height, except that the width of the letter "I" shall be equal to 1/6 of the letter height.

b. Letter stroke and spaces shall be equal to 1/6 the height, except that the space between "." (the period) and "A" shall be 1/3 letter height.

c. The space between "AIR" and "FORCE" shall be one letter width.

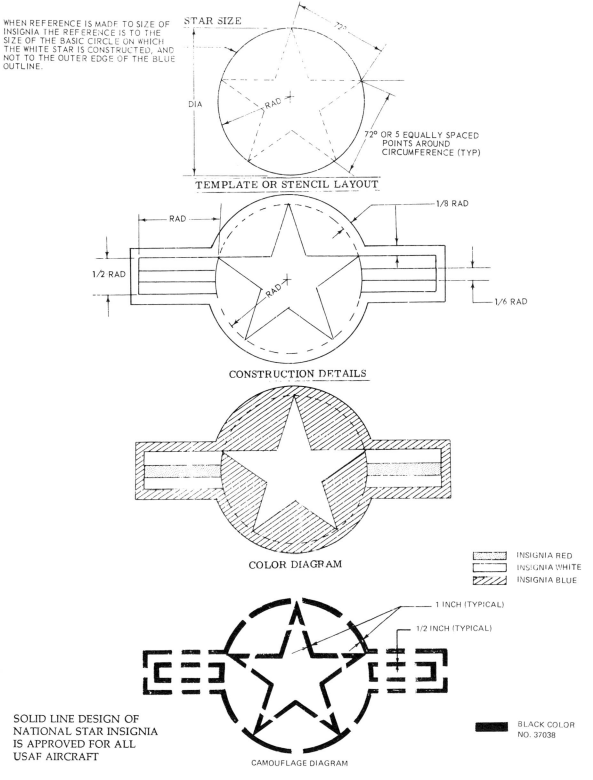

WHEN REFERENCE IS MADE TO SIZE OF INSIGNIA THE REFERENCE IS TO THE SIZE OF THE BASIC CIRCLE ON WHICH THE WHITE STAR IS CONSTRUCTED, AND NOT TO THE OUTER EDGE OF THE BLUE OUTLINE.

STAR SIZE

72°

DIA

RAD

72° OR 5 EQUALLY SPACED POINTS AROUND CIRCUMFERENCE (TYP)

TEMPLATE OR STENCIL LAYOUT

1/8 RAD

RAD

1/2 RAD

RAD

1/6 RAD

CONSTRUCTION DETAILS

COLOR DIAGRAM

INSIGNIA RED
INSIGNIA WHITE
INSIGNIA BLUE

1 INCH (TYPICAL)

1/2 INCH (TYPICAL)

BLACK COLOR NO. 37038

SOLID LINE DESIGN OF NATIONAL STAR INSIGNIA IS APPROVED FOR ALL USAF AIRCRAFT

CAMOUFLAGE DIAGRAM

Figure A-1. National Star Insignia

[The width of the red stripe has been misinterpreted on many USAF (and USN) aircraft since the red, white, and blue National Star Insignia came into use in 1947. The red stripe and the two white stripes should be the same width, with a thinner blue border; in some applications the red stripe is thinner, often as thin blue border; in a few rare applications the stripes and border are of equal width.]

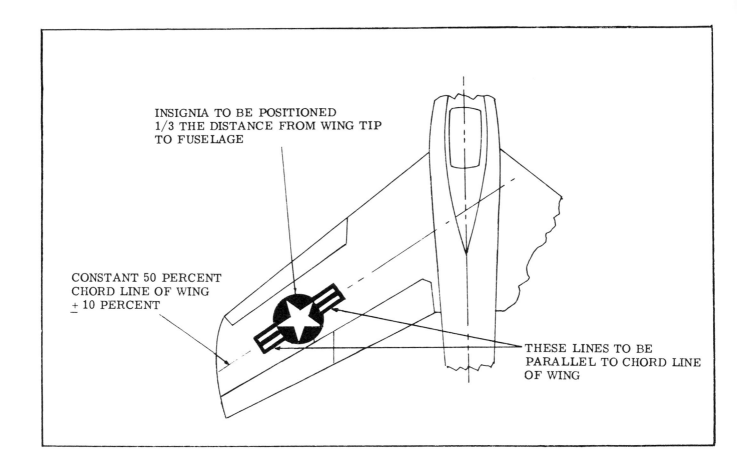

Figure A-2. National Star Insignia on Swept Wings

U.S. AIR FORCE
USAF

STENCILING EXAMPLE OF
AIRCRAFT MODEL DESIGNATION, SERIAL NUMBER AND FUEL REQUIREMENT

U.S. AIR FORCE _____ (MODEL DESIGNATION)

AF SERIAL NO. _____ A

SERVICE THIS AIRCRAFT WITH

GRADE _____

IDENTIPLATE LOCATION _____

_____

Figure A-3. "U.S. AIR FORCE," "USAF," and Aircraft Model
Designation, Serial Number, and Fuel Requirement

FORM OF LETTERS AND NUMERALS

SINGLE STROKE GOTHIC VERTICAL LETTERING

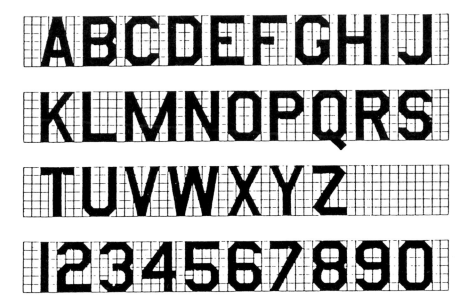

WIDTH OF LETTERS TO BE 2/3 OF HEIGHT
WIDTH OF LETTERS "M" AND "W" SAME AS HEIGHT
WIDTH OF LETTER "I" AND NUMERAL "1" TO BE 1/6 OF HEIGHT
STROKE TO BE 1/6 OF HEIGHT
SPACE BETWEEN LETTERS AND NUMERALS TO BE 1/6 OF HEIGHT
SPACE BETWEEN WORDS TO BE 2/3 OF HEIGHT

VERTICALLY APPLIED LETTERING:

SPACE BETWEEN LETTERS AND NUMERALS 1/6 HEIGHT
SPACE BETWEEN WORDS SAME AS HEIGHT

NOTE

THE USE OF HELVETICA LETTERING IS ACCEPTABLE.

Figure A-4. Form of Letters and Numerals

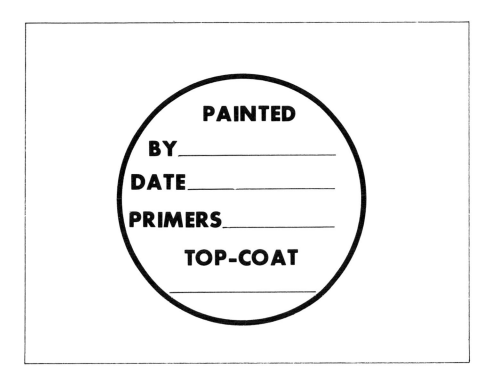

Figure A-5. Typical Marking for Identification
of Paint Shop and Applied Finish

APPENDIX B

USAF AIRCRAFT FINISH AND MARKING

SPECIFICATIONS AND ILLUSTRATIONS

NOTES:

1. THIS APPENDIX COVERS ONLY UNCAMOUFLAGED AIRCRAFT. SEE APPENDIX D FOR INFORMATION PERTAINING TO CAMOUFLAGED AIRCRAFT.

2. FORMER FINISH SYSTEM(S) WILL BE USED UNTIL REPLACEMENT IS REQUIRED (DUE TO DETERIORATION OR REMOVAL FOR INSPECTION). THE SYSTEM(S) WILL BE MAINTAINED BY TOUCH-UP, ETC., USING THE MATERIALS LISTED FOR THE SYSTEM. WHEN COMPLETE REPLACEMENT IS REQUIRED (DUE TO DETERIORATION OR REMOVAL FOR INSPECTION) THE STANDARD SYSTEM MATERIALS AS LISTED SHALL BE USED (SEE PARAGRAPH 2-2 FOR POLICY GUIDELINES).

C-5 AIRCRAFT MARKING SPECIFICATION (SEE FIG B-1)

1. MARKING	2. LOCATION	3. SIZE	4. COLOR NO/CODE
A U.S. AIR FORCE	Both sides of fuselage	Letters 24 inch high	15044
B Model Designation, Acft S/N and fuel Requirement	Left side of fuselage	Letters and numbers 1 inch high	17038
C National Star	Both sides of fuselage.	50 inch star	Background, border 15044, Stars and Bars - 17875, Stripes - 11136
D	On under surface of right wing and top surface of left wing	50 inch star	
E USAF	Top surface of right wing and under surface of left wing	50 inch high letters	15044
F Call Numbers		18 inch high numbers	17038
G Arctic Markings	One inch clearance around all large insignia and lettering		12197
H Walkway Border	Top both wings, fuselage and horizontal stabilizer	2 inches wide	17038
Anti-Glare			37038
I "MAC"	Each side VERT Fin	12 inch high letters	17875

C-5 AIRCRAFT EXTERIOR FINISHING SYSTEM

Area	PRESENT SYSTEM Color No.	System	STANDARD SYSTEM Color No.	System
All exterior areas except as specified			16473	MIL-C-83286
Battery Compartment			16473	MIL-C-83286
Landing Gear			17875	MIL-C-83286
Wheel Wells			17925	MIL-C-83286
Flap Wells			16473	MIL-C-83286
Radome			34092	MIL-C-83231, Type II
Relief Tube Areas			16473	MIL-C-83286
Walkways				
Engine Exhaust Path				
JJ White Caps as Required			17875	MIL-C-83286
Lower Fuselage				
APU Exhaust Paths				
Heater Exhaust Path				
Plastic Parts				

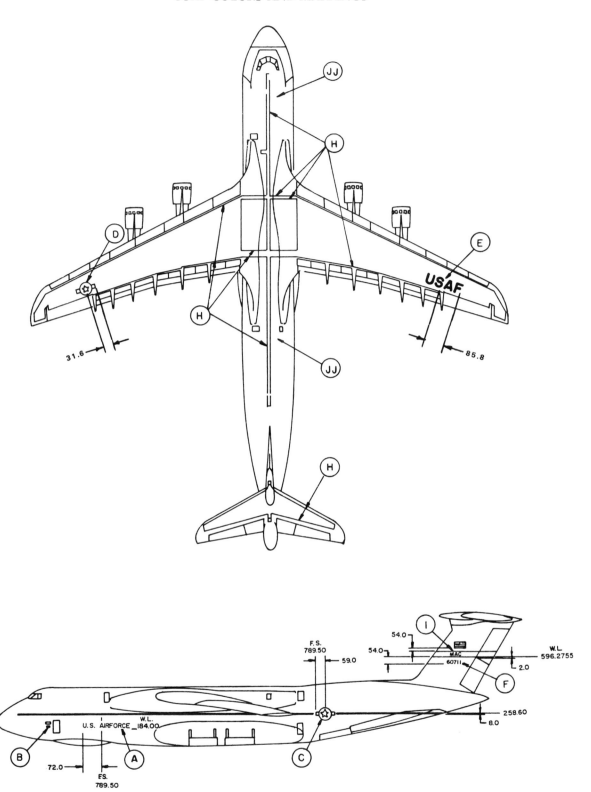

Figure B-1. C-5 Aircraft Marking Specification

[While the majority of regular Air Force C-5s are camouflaged, three or four 'white tops' are assigned to each wing. (The three regular C-5 wings are the 436th MAW at Dover AFB, Delaware, the 60th MAW at Travis AFB, California, and the 443d MAW at Altus AFB, Oklahoma.) All ANG C-5s are camouflaged.]

44

C-9 AIRCRAFT MARKING SPECIFICATION (SEE FIG B-2)

	1. MARKING	2. LOCATION	3. SIZE	4. COLOR NO/CODE
A	U. S AIR FORCE	Both sides of fuselage	Letters 24 inch high	15044
B	Model Designation, Acft S/N and fuel Requirement	Left side of fuselage	Letters and numbers 1 inch high	17038
C	National Star	Both sides of fuselage,	25 inch star	Background, border 15044, Stars and Bars - 17875, Stripes - 11136
D		On under surface of right wing and top surface of left wing	30 inch star	
E	USAF	Top surface of right wing and under surface of left wing	30 inch high letters	15044
F	Call Numbers	Both sides of vertical stabilizer	16 inch high numbers	17038
G	Arctic Markings			
H	Walkway Border	Top both wings in front	2 inches wide	17038
I	Anti-Glare	Top of fuselage in front of cockpit		37038

C-9 AIRCRAFT EXTERIOR FINISHING SYSTEM (SEE NOTE 2, PAGE 42)

Area	FORMER SYSTEM		STANDARD SYSTEM	
	Color No.	System	Color No.	System
All exterior areas except as specified	16473	MIL-L-19537	16473	MIL-C-83286
Battery Compartment	16473	MIL-C-38412	16473	MIL-C-83286
Landing Gear	16473	MIL-L-19537	16473	MIL-C-83286
Wheel Wells	16473	MIL-L-19537	16473	MIL-C-83286
Flap Wells				
Radome	17038	MIL-C-83231, Type II	17038	MIL-C-83231, Type II
Relief Tube Areas	16473	MIL-C-38412	16473	MIL-C-83286
Walkways				MIL-W-5044, Type I
Engine Exhaust Path	16473	MIL-C-38412	16473	MIL-C-83286
JJ White Caps as Required	17875	MIL-L-19537	17875	MIL-C-83286
Lower Fuselage			16473	
APU Exhaust Paths	16473	MIL-C-38412	16473	MIL-C-83286
Heater Exhaust Path	16473	MIL-C-38412	16473	MIL-C-83286
Plastic Parts	17038	MIL-C-83231, Type II	17038	MIL-C-83231, Type II
Horizontal Stab., Leading Edge			Bare	Bare
Vertical Stab., Leading Edge			Bare	Bare
Engine Pods, Leading Edge			Bare	Bare
Engine Pylons, Leading Edge			Bare	Bare
Wing, Leading Edge			Bare	Bare

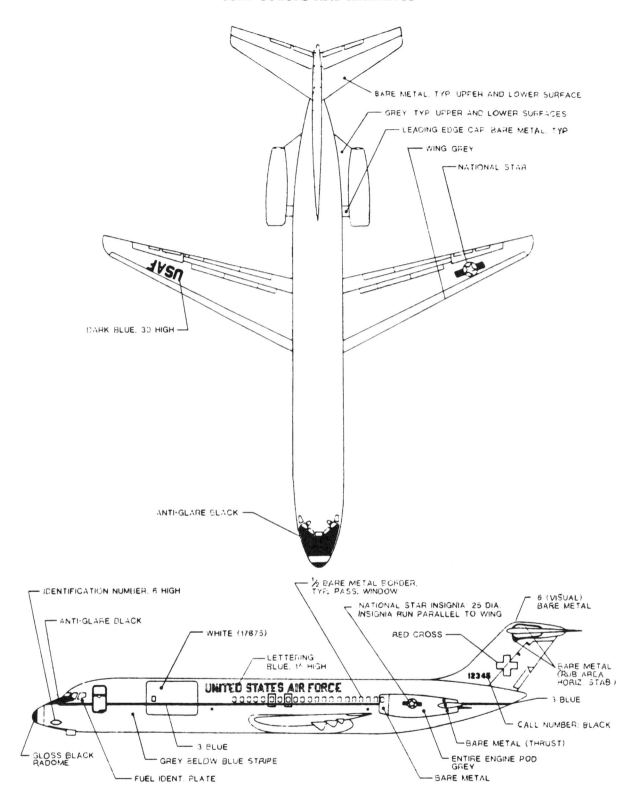

Figure B-2.   C-9[A] Aircraft Marking Specification

[Dated 24 December 1990, Change 34 of TO 1-1-4 brought C-9A marking specification drawings up to standards that had been in use since the 1970s. The white cap and three-inch cheat stripe were moved from just above to just below the cabin windows, and the "U.S. AIR FORCE" marking on the nose was replaced by a "UNITED STATES AIR FORCE" marking over the cabin windows.]

Border to white cap is (from top) 1" black, 3" gold, 1" black, and 9" medium blue
Base color is gray No. 16515, with unpainted metal leading edges to wings, tail, and nacelles
Forward lower fuselage sides unpainted metal
Vertical tail white. Gold chevron has 1/2" black piping. Lower chevron is medium blue

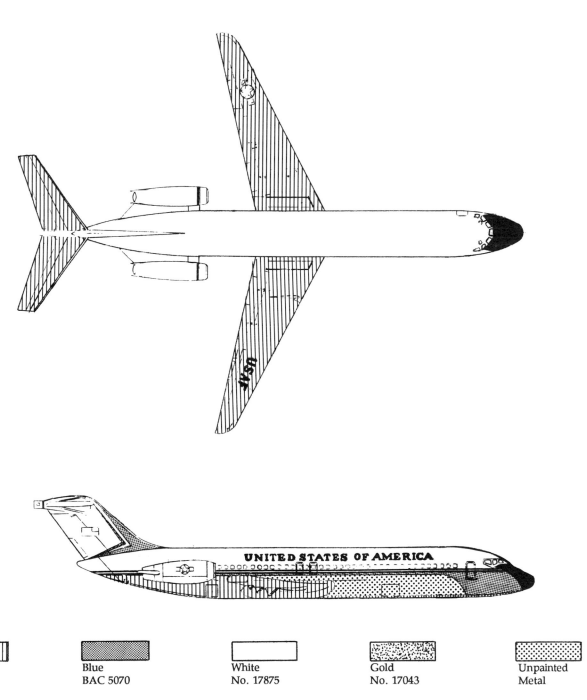

| Gray | Blue | White | Gold | Unpainted |
| No. 16515 | BAC 5070 | No. 17875 | No. 17043 | Metal |

[Figure B-3. C-9C Aircraft Marking Specification]

[The USAF's three C-9Cs are assigned to the 89th AW at Andrews AFB, Maryland.]

47

C-12 AIRCRAFT MARKING SPECIFICATION

1. MARKING	2. LOCATION	3. SIZE	4. COLOR NO./CODE
A. United States of America	Centered above wings on fuselage	Letters 6 inch high	17038
B. Model Designation, Act S/N, Fuel Requirement	Left side of fuselage	1 inch high letters and numbers	17038
C. National Star	Both sides of fuselage upper surface on left wing, lower surface on right wing	16 inch star	Background, border - 15044 Stars and bars - 17875 Stripes - 11136
D. USAF	Upper surface - right wing Lower surface - left wing	20 inch high letters	17038
E. Call numbers	Both sides of vertical stabilizer	8 inch high numbers	17038
F. Arctic Markings			
G. Walking Border			
H. Anti-Glare	Top fuselage forward of cockpit Inboard side of nacelle		37038 37038
I. Propeller Tips	Forward side	4 inches from tip	13538
J. U.S. Flag	Centered both sides of vertical tail	13 inches high	
K. Fuselage Lines	Both side of fuselage (tapered) Beginning at FS 14,000 running horizontally to tail		17038 17043
L. Engine Nacelle	Both sides of nacelle (tapered) Beginning approximately FS 80 running horizontally to nacelle end		17038 17043

C-12 AIRCRAFT EXTERIOR FINISHING SYSTEM

Area	FORMER SYSTEM Color No.	System	STANDARD SYSTEM Color No.	System
All exterior areas except as specified			17875	MIL-C-83286
Battery Compartment			17875	MIL-C-83286
Landing Gear			17875	MIL-C-83286
Wheel Wells			17875	MIL-C-83286
Flap Wells			17875	MIL-C-83286
Radome				
Relief Tube Areas				
Walkways				
Engine Exhaust Path				
White Caps as Required				
APU Exhaust Paths				
Heater Exhaust Path				
Plastic Parts				
Aileron Wells			17875	MIL-C-83286
MM Lower Fuselage Surface to Blue			16473	MIL-C-83286
NN Lower Outboard Engine Nacelle			16473	MIL-C-83286
OO Forward Lower Fuselage to Gray			15090	MIL-C-83286
PP Middle Engine Nacelle			16473	MIL-C-83286

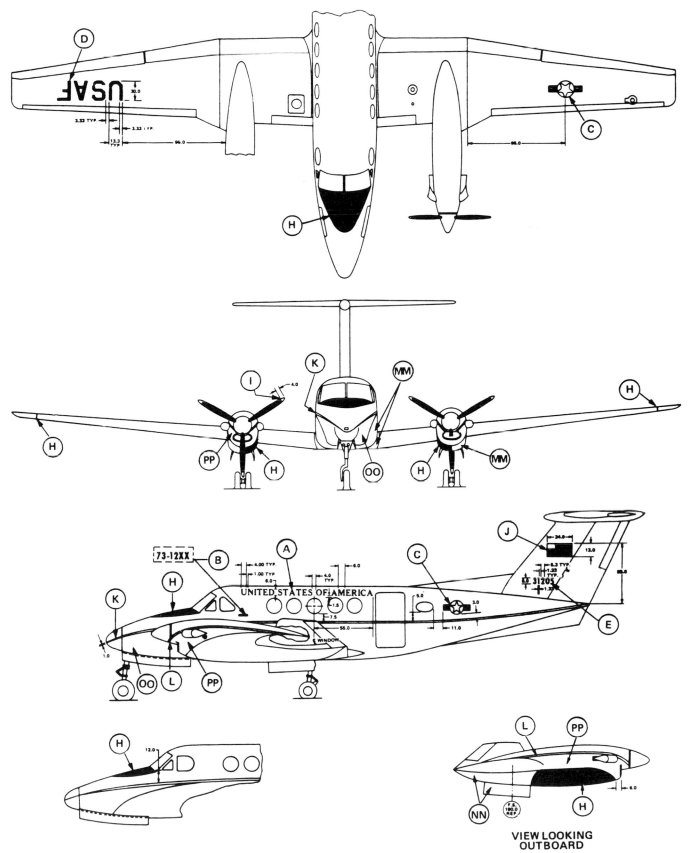

Figure B-4. C-12 Aircraft Marking Specification

Overall Insignia White 17875
Fuselage and wing tank stripes Insignia Blue 15044
"USAF," "UNITED STATES AIR FORCE," and radio call
    number in Insignia Blue 15044
Leading edges of wings, stabilizers, and nacelles
    left unpainted metal

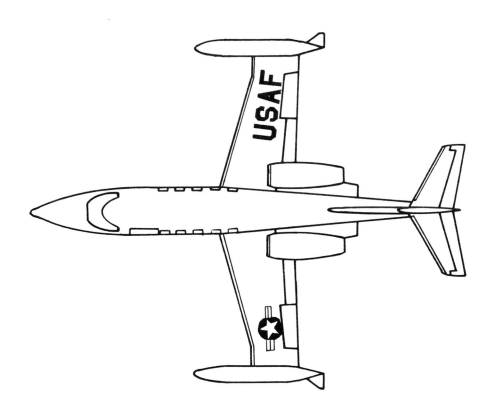

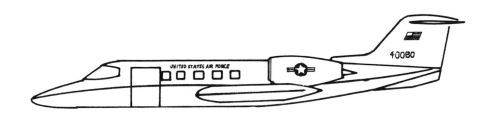

[Figure B-5. C-21A Paint Scheme]
[USAF Serial Numbers 84-0063 through 84-0080]

Overall Insignia White 17875
Fuselage and wing tank stripes Insignia Blue 15044
"UNITED STATES OF AMERICA" and radio call number
   in Insignia Blue 15044
Leading edges of wings, stabilizers, and nacelles
   left unpainted metal

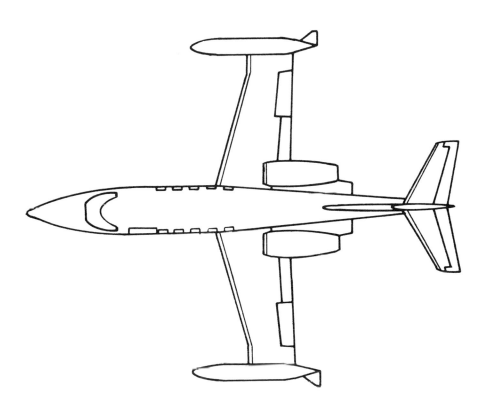

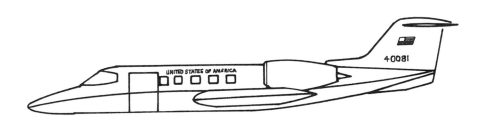

[Figure B-6. C-21A Paint Scheme (Diplomatic)]
[USAF Serial Numbers 84-0081 through 84-0086]

"UNITED STATES OF AMERICA" in Black on Fuselage Side
"USAF" in Dark Blue BAC 5070 above right wing and below left wing
Leading edges of wings, tail, and nacelles are unpainted metal

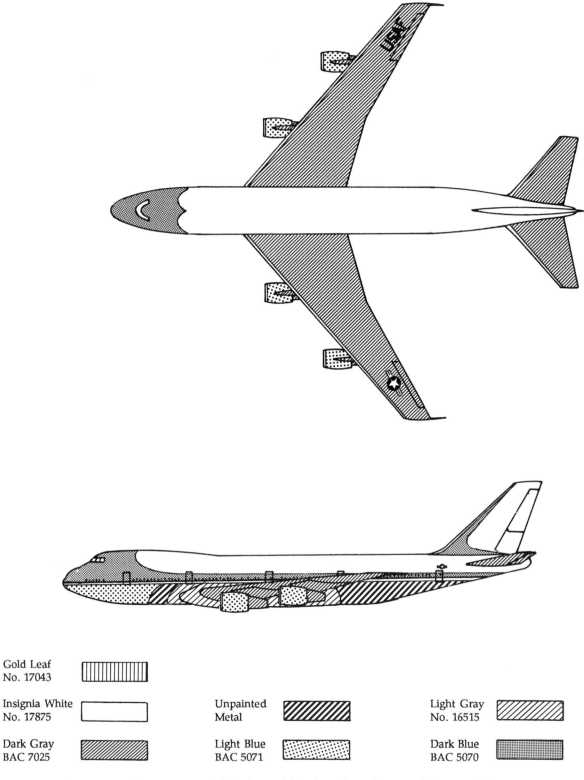

Gold Leaf
No. 17043

Insignia White   Unpainted   Light Gray
No. 17875   Metal   No. 16515

Dark Gray   Light Blue   Dark Blue
BAC 7025   BAC 5071   BAC 5070

[Figure B-7. C-25A Aircraft Marking Specification (Sheet 1 of 2)]

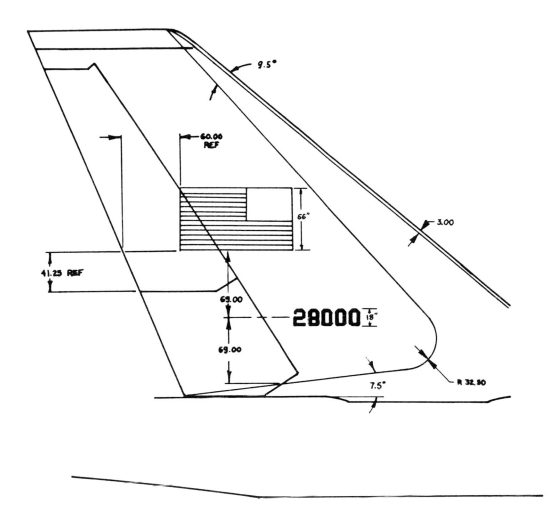

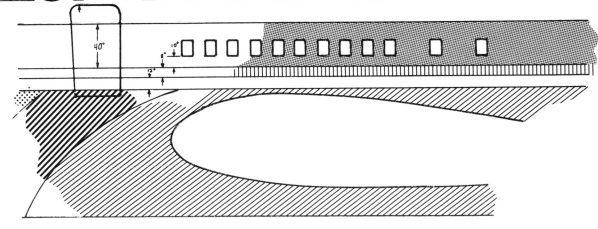

[Figure B-7. C-25A Aircraft Marking Specification (Sheet 2 of 2)]

C-130 AIRCRAFT MARKING SPECIFICATION (SEE FIG B-8)

1. MARKING	2. LOCATION	3. SIZE	4. COLOR NO/CODE
A U.S. AIR FORCE	Both sides of fuselage	Letters 20 inch high	15044
B Model Designation, Acft S/N and fuel Requirement	Left side of fuselage	Letters and numbers 1 inch high	17038
C National Star	Both sides of fuselage	50 inch star	Background, border - 15044, Stars and Bars - 17875, Stripes - 11136
D	On under surface of right wing and top surface of left wing		
E USAF	Top surface of right wing and under surface of left wing	50 inch high letters	15044
F Call Numbers	Both sides of vertical stabilizer	18 inch high letters	17038
G Arctic Markings	One inch clearance around all large insignia and lettering		12197
H Anti-Glare	N/A		37038
I Propeller Caution Band	On fuselage through same plane of propeller travel	3 inches wide	Band Arrows; Danger - 11136 Propeller 17875
J Propeller Tips	On both sides	*4 inches to tip	33538
K Walkway Border	Top of wing, fuselage and stabilizer	2 inches wide	17038

*NOTE: Propellers 15 feet and over in diameter require 6 inch yellow tip.

C-130 AIRCRAFT EXTERIOR FINISHING SYSTEM (SEE NOTE 2, PAGE 42)

Area	FORMER SYSTEM		STANDARD SYSTEM	
	Color No.	System	Color No.	System
All exterior areas except as specified	17178	MIL-L-19537	16473	MIL-C-83286
Battery Compartment	17038	TT-L-54	16473	MIL-C-83286
Landing Gear	17178	MIL-L-19537	17875	MIL-C-83286
Wheel Wells	17178	Corrogard 14	17178 ***	MIL-C-83286
Flap Wells	17178	TT-P-28	16473	MIL-C-83286
Radome	17038	MIL-C-7439, Class II	17038	MIL-C-83231, Type II
Relief Tube Areas	17038	TT-L-54	16473 & 17038	MIL-C-83286
HH Walkways		MIL-W-5044, Type I		MIL-W-5044, Type II
II Engine Exhaust Path	17875	MIL-C-27227	16473	MIL-C-83286
JJ White Caps as Required	17875	MIL-L-19537	17875	MIL-C-83286
Lower Fuselage				
APU Exhaust Paths				
Heater Exhaust Path				
Plastic Parts				
OO Upper Wing Panels	36231	MIL-C-38713	36231	*MIL-C-81733, Type III
Pitot Tube Support Surface			16473	**MIL-C-83286

*System consists of 1 coat of MIL-C-81706, 1 coat of PR 1432G, 1 coat of PR 1436G, 1 coat of PR 1436AS. MIL-C-83286 overcoat when required to match color.

**
1. Clean, corrosion treat, and prepare pitot tube support surface in accordance with TO's 1-1-1, 1-1-2, and 1-1-8.

2. Apply a coating of PR-1432G corrosion inhibited primer, National Stock No. 8030-00-433-9032, to a thickness of 3-5 mils.

3. Allow PR-1432G to dry to a tack free condition and overcoat with MIL-C-83286 polyurethane paint to a thickness of 2 mils in accordance with TO 1-1-8.

***4. Optional color No. 36622, MIL-C-83286.

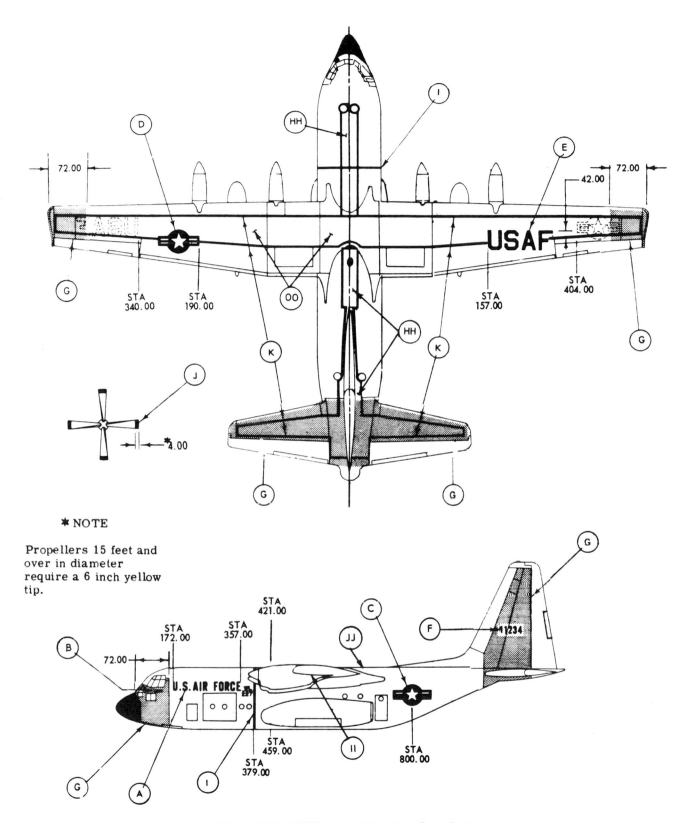

Figure B-8. C-130 Aircraft Marking Specification

★ NOTE

Propellers 15 feet and over in diameter require a 6 inch yellow tip.

[Although nearly all C-130s are camouflaged, this overall gray scheme is used by the four AFRES WC-130s, and a few C-130s assigned for mission support of Air National Guard units. AFSC also operates at least two white-capped C-130s in test programs.]

C-135 AIRCRAFT MARKING SPECIFICATION (SEE FIG B-9)

	1. MARKING	2. LOCATION	3. SIZE	4. COLOR NO/CODE
A	U. S AIR FORCE	Both sides of fuselage	Letters 30 inch high	15044
B	Model Designation, Acft S/N and fuel Requirement	Left side of fuselage	Letters and numbers 1 inch high	17038
C	National Star	Both sides of fuselage		Background, border - 15044, Stars and Bars - 17875, Stripes - 11136
D		On under surface of right wing and top surface of left wing	50 inch star	
E	USAF	Top surface of right wing and under surface of left wing	55 inch high letters	15044
F	Call Numbers	Both sides of vertical stabilizer	18 inch high numbers	17038
G	Arctic Markings	One inch clearance around all large insignia and lettering		12197
H	Anti-Glare	Top of fuselage in front of cockpit		37038

C-135 AIRCRAFT EXTERIOR FINISHING SYSTEM (SEE NOTE 2, PAGE 42)

Area	FORMER SYSTEM		STANDARD SYSTEM	
	Color No.	System	Color No.	System
All exterior areas except as specified	17178	MIL-C-83151	16473	MIL-C-83286
Battery Compartment	17038	MIL-C-7439, Class I	16473	MIL-C-83286
Landing Gear	17178		17875	MIL-C-83286
Wheel Wells	YELLOW	MIL-P-8585	16473	MIL-C-83286
Flap Wells	YELLOW	MIL-P-8585	16473	MIL-C-83286
Radome	17038	MIL-C-7439, Class II	17038	MIL-C-83231, Type II
Relief Tube Areas			16473	MIL-C-83286
Walkways				
Engine Exhaust Path			16473	MIL-C-83286
White Caps as Required			17875	MIL-C-83286
Lower Fuselage				
APU Exhaust Paths			16473	MIL-C-83286
Heater Exhaust Path			16473	MIL-C-83286
Plastic Parts			17038	MIL-C-83231, Type II

NOTE: Special purpose C-135 Aircraft may be painted
with color No. 16473.

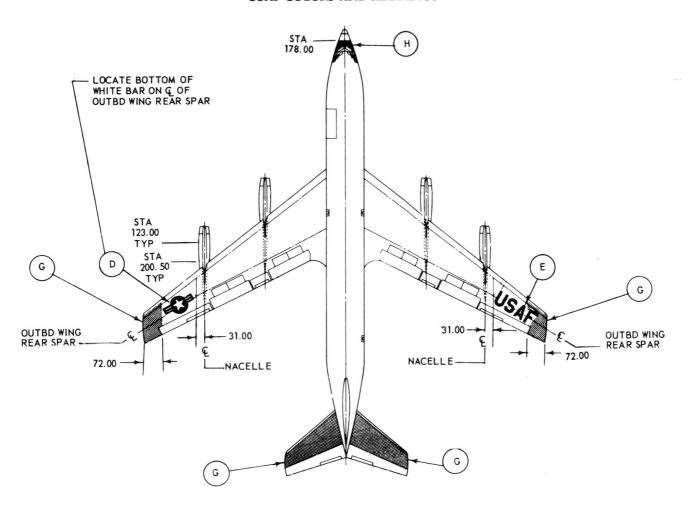

TOP VIEW

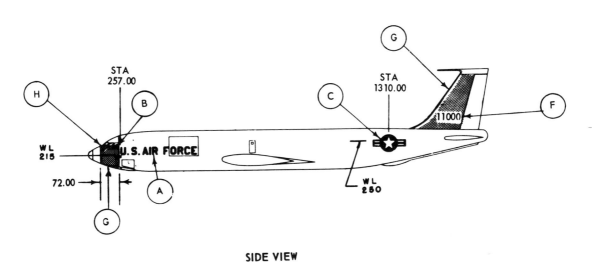

SIDE VIEW

Figure B-9. C-135 Aircraft Marking Specification

C-141 AIRCRAFT MARKING SPECIFICATION (SEE FIG B-10)

1. MARKING	2. LOCATION	3. SIZE	4. COLOR NO/CODE
A U.S. AIR FORCE	Both sides of fuselage	Letters 21 inch high	15044
B Model Designation, Acft S/N and fuel Requirement	Left side of fuselage	Letters and numbers 1 inch high	17038
C National Star	Both sides of fuselage	50 inch star	Background, border - 15044, Stars and Bars - 17875, Stripes - 11136
D	On under surface of right wing and top surface of left wing		
E USAF	Top surface of right wing and under surface of left wing	50 inch high letters	15044
F Call Numbers	Both sides of vertical stabilizer	18 inch high numbers	17038
G Arctic Markings	One inch clearance around all large insignia and lettering		12197
H Walkway Border		2 inches wide	17038
Anti-Glare	N/A		37038

C-141 AIRCRAFT EXTERIOR FINISHING SYSTEM (SEE NOTE 2, PAGE 42)

Area	FORMER SYSTEM		STANDARD SYSTEM	
	Color No.	System	Color No.	System
All exterior areas except as specified	17178	MIL-L-19537	16473	MIL-C-83286
Battery Compartment	16473	MIL-E-15936	16473	MIL-C-83286
Landing Gear	17875	MIL-C-27227	17875	MIL-C-83286*
Wheel Wells	17875	Corrogard 25	16473	MIL-C-83286
Leading Edges	BARE	BARE	16473	MIL-C-83286
Flap Wells	17178	MIL-L-19537	16473	MIL-C-83286
Radome	17038	MIL-L-7439, Class I	17038	MIL-C-83231, Type II
Relief Tube Areas	17178	Corrogard	16473	MIL-C-83286
Walkways				MIL-W-5044, Type I
Engine Exhaust Path				
JJ White Caps as Required	17875	MIL-L-19537	17875	MIL-C-83286
Lower Fuselage				
APU Exhaust Paths				
Heater Exhaust Path				
Plastic Parts				
Engine Ring Cowl			BARE	BARE
Lighting Deflectors			BARE	BARE
Doppler Antenna Covers			BARE	BARE
Wing Ram Air Scoops			BLACK	MIL-C-83231, Type II

*See applicable 4S Series technical orders for appropriate finish and/or materials.

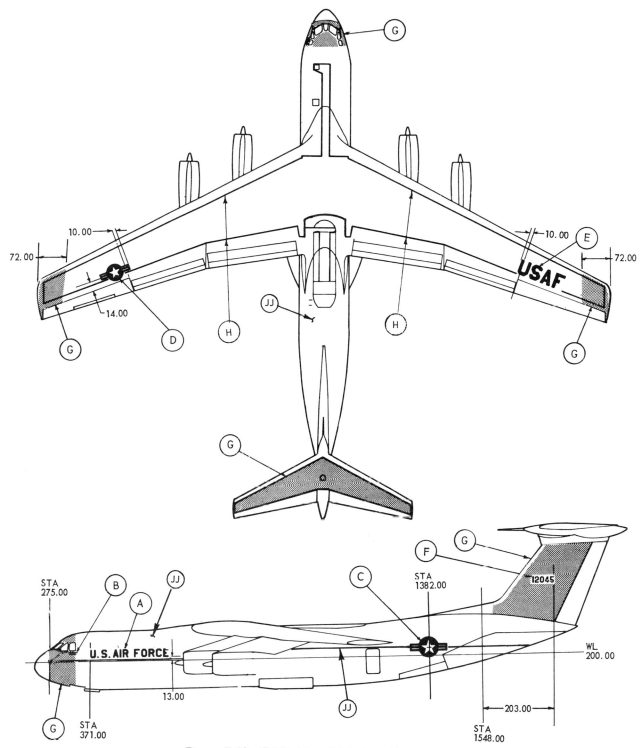

Figure B-10. C-141 Aircraft Marking Specification

[The majority of C-141As have been stretched and modified into C-141Bs; the four remaining 141As are assigned to AFSC for systems testing. The "white tops" comprise the AFSC aircraft and two or three C-141s in each regular Air Force wing (the 60th MAW at Travis AFB, California, 62d MAW at McChord AFB, Washington, the 63d MAW at Norton AFB, California, 437th MAW at Charleston AFB, South Carolina, the 438th MAW at McGuire AFB, New Jersey, and the 443d MAW at Altus AFB, Oklahoma). All remaining regular Air Force, AFRES, and ANG C-141s are camouflaged.]

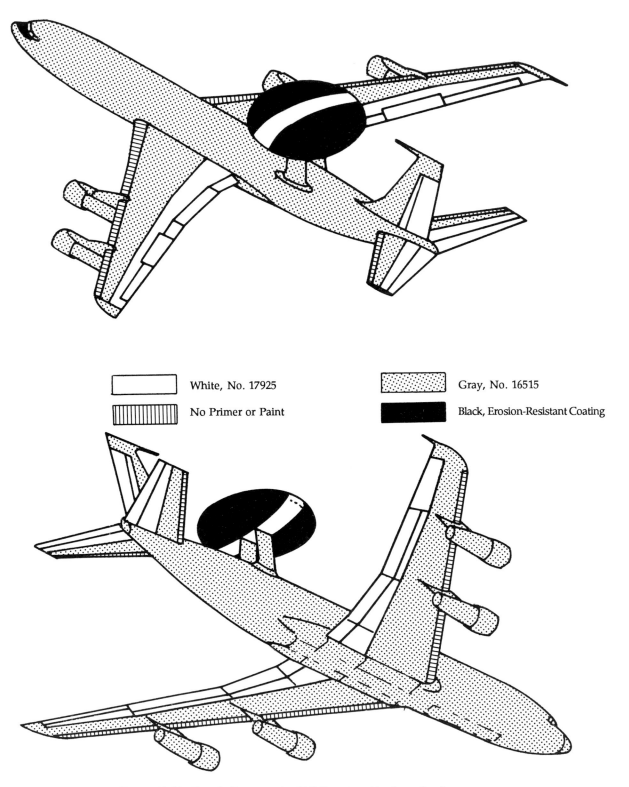

Figure B-11. Finish Systems for E-3 Exterior Airplane Surfaces

[Note that the E-3's base color is 16515 Boeing Gray, rather than the standard Air Force 16473.]

Overall BAC 7067 White
40" Fuselage stripe Blue No. 35231
US Flag on tail is placed as on C-25 (see page 51)
"UNITED STATES OF AMERICA" fuselage marking as on C-25 (see page 51)

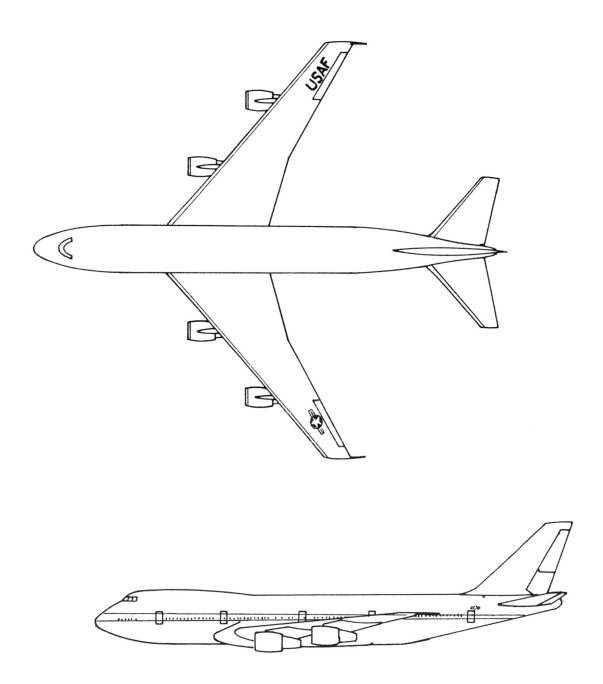

[Figure B-12. Finish Systems for E-4 Exterior Airplane Surfaces]

H-1 AIRCRAFT MARKING SPECIFICATION (SEE FIG B-13)

1. MARKING	2. LOCATION	3. SIZE	4. COLOR NO/CODE
A U.S. AIR FORCE	Both sides of fuselage	Letters 6 inch high	15044
B Model Designation, Acft S/N and fuel Requirement	Left side of fuselage	Letters and numbers 1 inch high	17038
C National Star	Both sides of fuselage	16 inch star	Background, border - 15044, Stars and Bars - 17875, Stripes - 11136
D	Located on underside of fuselage		
E	On upper surface of fuselage		
F Call Numbers	Both sides of tailboom	6 inch high numbers	17038
G Anti-Glare	Top of fuselage in front of cockpit		37038
H Walkway Border	Top of fuselage	2 inches wide	17038
I Arctic Markings	N/A		12197
J Rotor Warning	Both sides of fuselage	2 inch high letters	See Para 6-13 and Figure E-5

H-1 AIRCRAFT EXTERIOR FINISHING SYSTEM (SEE NOTE 2, PAGE 42)

Area	FORMER SYSTEM		STANDARD SYSTEM	
	Color No.	System	Color No.	System
All exterior areas except as specified	15045	MIL-L-19537	16473	MIL-C-83286
Battery Compartment	17038	MIL-C-7439, Class I	16473	MIL-C-83286
Landing Gear	15045	MIL-L-19537	16473	MIL-C-83286
Wheel Wells				
Flap Wells				
Radome			17038	MIL-C-83231, Type II
Relief Tube Areas			16473	MIL-C-83286
HH Walkways				MIL-W-5044, Type I
Engine Exhaust Path			16473	MIL-C-83286
White Caps as Required			17875	MIL-C-83286
Lower Fuselage				
APU Exhaust Paths				
Heater Exhaust Path				
Plastic Parts			17038	MIL-C-83231, Type II
Upper Fuselage	17875	MIL-L-19537	16473	MIL-C-83286
* PP Top surface of main rotor blade	34087	MIL-L-81352	37038	MIL-C-83286
* QQ Bottom surface of main rotor blade	37038	MIL-L-81352	37038	MIL-C-83286
* Tail Rotor Blades			37038	MIL-C-83286

* Rotor blade painting at maintenance level is limited to touch-
up of minor repairs.

62

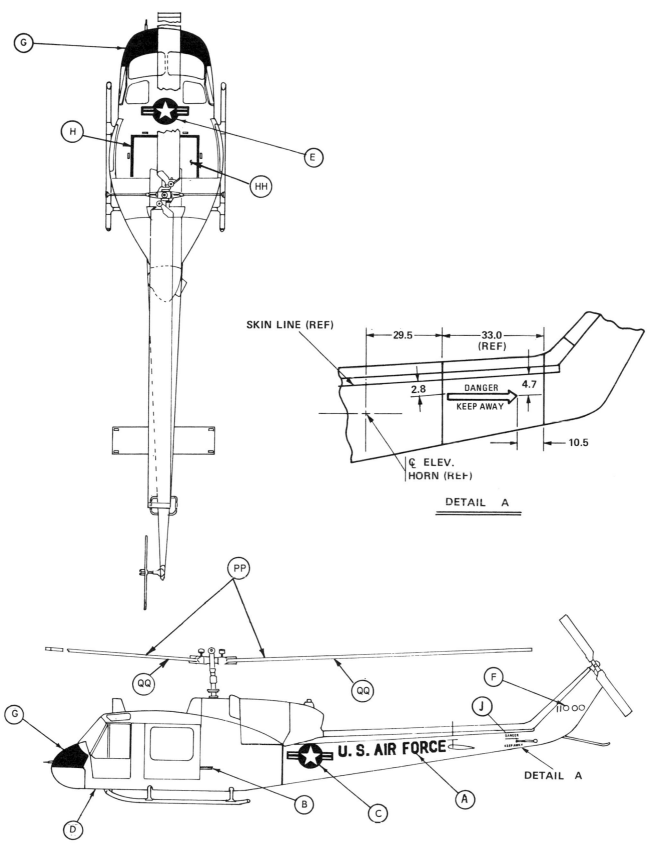

Figure B-13. H-1 Aircraft Marking Specification

Fuselage is Insignia Blue No. 15044
Fuselage stripe is 5" Gold No. 17043 with 1/2" black piping inside 1/4" white piping
White cap is Insignia White No. 17875
White cap border is 1-1/2" Gold No. 17043 with 1/4" black piping above, 1/4" black and 1/4" white piping below

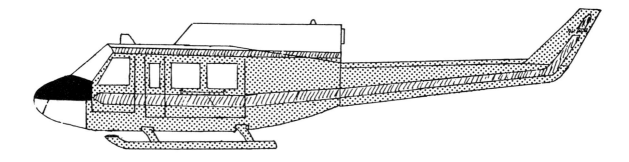

[Figure B-14. UH-1N Aircraft Marking Specification (89th AW)]

T-37 AIRCRAFT MARKING SPECIFICATION (SEE FIG B-15)

	1. MARKING	2. LOCATION	3. SIZE	4. COLOR NO./CODE
A	U.S. AIR FORCE	Both sides of fuselage	Letters 6 inch high	17875
B	Model Designation, Acft S/N Fuel Requirement	Single point refueling	Characters 3/8 inch Characters 3/8 inch Characters 1/4 inch	17875 White on blue
C	National Star	Both sides of fuselage	15 inch star	Background,
D		On under surface of right wing and top surface of left wing	30 inch star	border - 15044, Stars and Bars - 17875, Stripes - 11136
E	USAF	Top surface of right wing and under surface of left wing	30 inch high letters	17875
F	Call Numbers	Both sides of vertical stabilizer	6 inch high numbers	17875
H	Anti-Glare	Top of fuselage in front of cockpit		37038
I	Walkway Border	Top of wings	2 inches wide	15044
J	Cockpit Access Step Door	Both sides of fuselage just forward of wing leading edge	Entire door	15044

T-37 AIRCRAFT EXTERIOR FINISHING SYSTEM (SEE NOTE 2, PAGE 42)

Area	STANDARD SYSTEM	
	Color No.	System
All exterior areas except as specified	TOP FUSELAGE 17875 BOTTOM FUSELAGE 15044	MIL-C-83286
Battery Compartment	17875	MIL-C-83286
Landing Gear	17875	MIL-C-83286
Wheel Wells	17875	MIL-C-83286
Flap Wells	15044	MIL-C-83286
Radome		
Relief Tube Areas		
HH Walkway		MIL-W-5044, Type I
Engine Exhaust Path	15044	MIL-C-83286
White Caps as Required	17875	MIL-C-83286
Lower Fuselage	15044	
APU Exhaust Paths		
Heater Exhaust Path		
Plastic Parts		

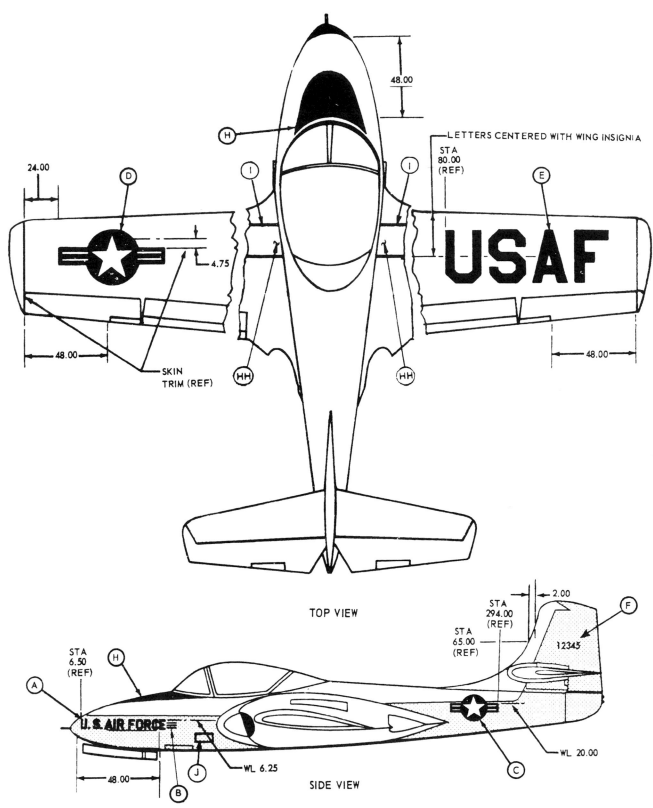

Figure B-15. T-37 Aircraft Marking Specification

[Although ATC is repainting all T-37s in this blue and white scheme, many aircraft remain in the all-white scheme introduced in the 1970s.]

T-38 AIRCRAFT MARKING SPECIFICATION (SEE FIG B-16)

	1. MARKING	2. LOCATION	3. SIZE	4. COLOR NO/CODE
A	U.S. AIR FORCE	Both sides of fuselage	Letters 12 inch high	15044
B	Model Designation, Acft S/N Fuel Requirement	Single point refueling	Characters 5/8 inch Characters 5/8 inch Characters 3/8 inch	15044 Blue on white
C	National Star	Both sides of fuselage	20 inch star	Background,
D		On under surface of right wing and top surface of left wing	20 inch star	border - 15044, Stars and Bars - 17875, Stripes - 11136
E	USAF	Top surface of right wing and under surface of left wing	22.5 inch high letters	15044
F	Call Numbers	Both sides of vertical stabilizer	12 inch high numbers	15044
G	Arctic Markings (Not Authorized for ATC Aircraft)	One inch clearance around all large insignia and letter-ing		12197
H	Anti-Glare	Top of fuselage in front of cockpit		37038

T-38 AIRCRAFT EXTERIOR FINISHING SYSTEM (SEE NOTE 2, PAGE 42)

Area	STANDARD SYSTEM	
	Color No.	System
All exterior areas except as specified	17875	MIL-C-83286
Battery Compartment	17875	MIL-C-83286
Landing Gear	17875	MIL-C-83286
Wheel Wells	17875	MIL-C-83286
Flap Wells	17875	MIL-C-83286
Radome	17038	MIL-C-83231, Type II
Relief Tube Areas		
Walkways		
Engine Exhaust Path		
White Caps as Required		
Lower Fuselage		
APU Exhaust Paths		
Heater Exhaust Path		
Plastic Parts		
Leading Edge of Vertical Stabilizer	17875	MIL-C-83231, Type II
Inboard Ends of Vertical Stabilizer	17875	MIL-C-83286
Trailing Edge of Vertical Stabilizer	17875	MIL-C-83286

67

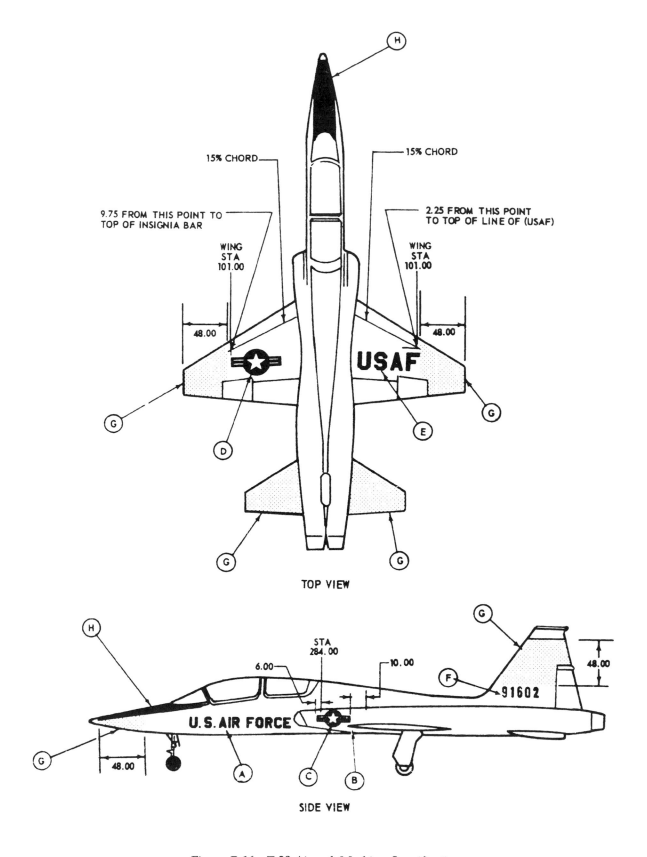

TOP VIEW

15% CHORD

15% CHORD

9.75 FROM THIS POINT TO
TOP OF INSIGNIA BAR

2.25 FROM THIS POINT
TO TOP OF LINE OF (USAF)

WING
STA
101.00

WING
STA
101.00

48.00

48.00

USAF

SIDE VIEW

STA
284.00

6.00

10.00

91602

48.00

U.S. AIR FORCE

48.00

Figure B-16. T-38 Aircraft Marking Specification

T-39 AIRCRAFT MARKING SPECIFICATION (SEE FIG B-17)

1. MARKING		2. LOCATION	3. SIZE	4. COLOR NO/CODE
A	U.S. AIR FORCE	Both sides of fuselage	Letters 12 inch high	15044
B	Model Designation. Acft S/N and Fuel Requirement	Left side of fuselage	Letters and numbers 1 inch high	17038
C	National Star	Both sides of fuselage	20 inch star	Background,
D		On under surface of right wing and top surface of left wing	30 inch star	border - 15044, Stars and Bars - 17875, Stripes - 11136
E	USAF	Top surface of right wing and under surface of left wing	30 inch high letters	15044
F	Call Numbers	Both sides of vertical stabilizer rudder	12 inch high numbers	17038
G	Arctic Markings	One inch clearance around all large insignia and lettering		12197
I	Walkway Border	Top of wings and engine pylons	2 inches wide	37038

T-39 AIRCRAFT EXTERIOR FINISHING SYSTEM (SEE NOTE 2, PAGE 42)

Area	FORMER SYSTEM		STANDARD SYSTEM	
	Color No.	System	Color No.	System
All exterior areas except as specified	17875	Jet Skin No. 171-W-562/ MIL-L-19537	16473	MIL-C-83286
Battery Compartment	17875	Ever Lube 13-511	17875	MIL-C-83286
Landing Gear	17178	MIL-P-19537	17875	MIL-C-83286
Wheel Wells	YELLOW	MIL-P-8585	17875	MIL-C-83286
Flap Wells	YELLOW	MIL-P-8585	16473	MIL-C-83286
Radome	17038	MIL-C-7439, Class II	17038	MIL-C-83231, Type II
Relief Tube Areas				
HH Walkways *	36440	MIL-W-5044 Type I	37038	MIL-W-5044, Type II
Engine Exhaust Path			16473	MIL-C-83286
JJ White Caps as Required			17875	MIL-C-83286
Lower Fuselage	17178	Jet Skin No. 171-A27/ MIL-L-19537	16473	MIL-C-83286
APU Exhaust Paths				
Heater Exhaust Path				
Plastic Parts				
Aileron Wells			16473	MIL-C-83286
Vertical Stabilizer Tip			17038	MIL-C-83231, Type II

*Note: Apply Anti-skid coating to within 2″ of engine nacelle.

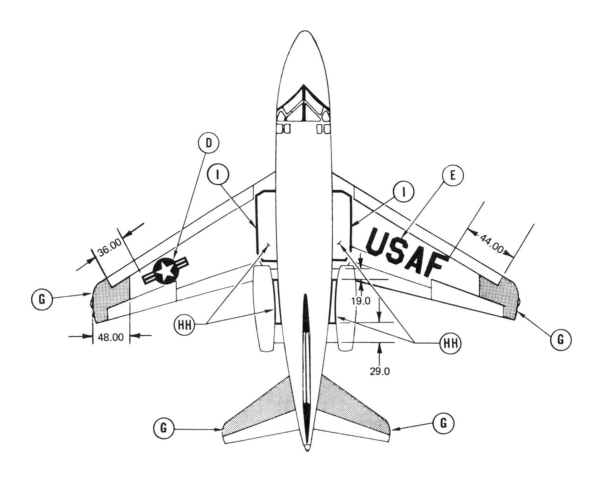

TOP VIEW

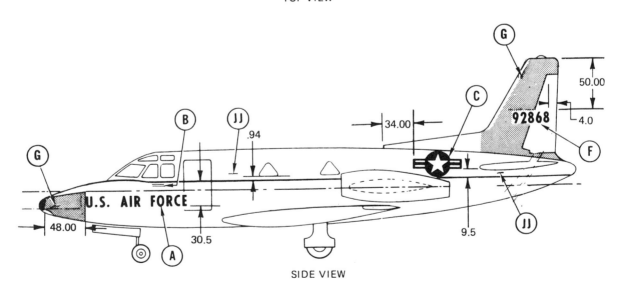

SIDE VIEW

Figure B-17. T-39 Aircraft Marking Specification

[While the USAF has retired most T-39s and CT-39s, AFSC's 4950th Test Wing retains a few in this scheme for systems testing.]

T-39 ALL-WHITE AIRCRAFT MARKING SPECIFICATION (SEE FIG B-18)

1.	MARKING	2. LOCATION	3. SIZE	4. COLOR NO/CODE
A	UNITED STATES AIR FORCE	Both sides	Letters 6 inches high	15044
B	National Star	Centered outb'd side of both engine nacelles. Nacelle Sta. 119.4	15 inch star	N/A
C	Call Numbers	Both sides of vertical stabilizer rudder	8 inch high numbers	15044
D	U.S. Flag	Centered both sides of vertical stabilizer, Sta. 59.8	11 inches	N/A
E	Fuselage Separation Line	Both sides of fuselage, beginning at Sta. 90.5 (tapered around crew compartment window) running horizontally to tail, 2 inches below fuselage windows	2 inches wide	15044
F	Anti-Glare	Top fuselage forward of cockpit	Apply in accordance with AF Drawing 8123670	37038

T-39 ALL-WHITE AIRCRAFT EXTERIOR FINISHING SYSTEM (SEE NOTE 2, PAGE 42)

Area	FORMER SYSTEM		STANDARD SYSTEM	
	Color No.	System	Color No.	System
All exterior areas except as Specified	17875	Jet Skin No. 171-W-562 MIL-L-19537	17875	MIL-C-83286
Battery Compartment	17875	Ever Lube 13-511	17875	MIL-C-83286
Landing Gear	17178	MIL-P-19537	17875	MIL-C-83286
Wheel Wells	YELLOW	MIL-P-8585	17875	MIL-C-83286
Flap Wells	YELLOW	MIL-P-8585	17875	MIL-C-83286
Radome	17038	MIL-C-7439, Class II	17038	MIL-C-83231, Type II
Relief Tube Areas				
HH Walkways *	36440	MIL-W-5044, Type I	37038	MIL-W-5044, Type II
Engine Exhaust Path			17875	MIL-C-83286
JJ White Caps as Required			17875	MIL-C-83286
Lower Fuselage	17178	Jet Skin No. 171-A27 MIL-L-19537	17875	MIL-C-83286
APU Exhaust Paths				
Heater Exhaust Path				
Plastic Parts				
Aileron Wells			17875	MIL-C-83286
Vertical Stabilizer Tip			17875	MIL-C-83206

* Note: Apply Anti-skid coating to within 2" of engine nacelle.

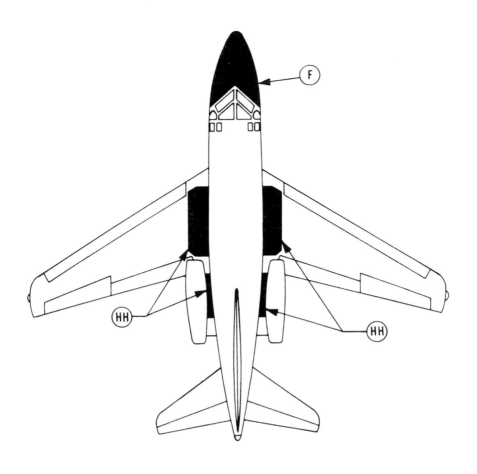

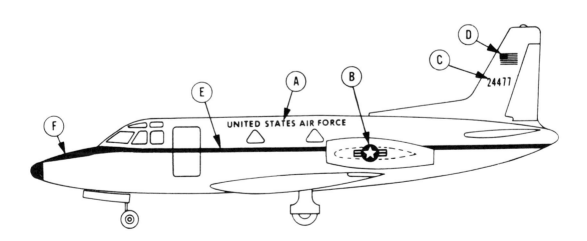

Figure B-18. T-39 All-White Aircraft Marking Specification

[While the USAF has retired most T-39s and CT-39s, AFSC's 4950th Test Wing retains a few in this scheme for systems testing.]

T-41 AIRCRAFT MARKING SPECIFICATION (SEE FIG B-19)

	1. MARKING	2. LOCATION	3. SIZE	4. COLOR NO/CODE
A	U.S. AIR FORCE	Both sides of fuselage	Letters 6 inch high	15044
B	Model Designation, Acft S/N and fuel Requirement	Left side of fuselage	Letters and numbers 1 inch high	17038
C	National Star	On under surface of right wing and top surface of left wing	20 inch star	Background, border - 15044, Stars and Bars - 17875, Stripes - 11136
D	USAF	Top surface of right wing and under surface of left wing	20 inch high letters	15044
E	Call Numbers	Both sides of vertical stabilizer	6 inch high numbers	17038
F	Arctic Markings	One inch clearance around all large insignia and lettering		12197
H	Anti-Glare	On fuselage in front of cockpit		37038
I	FAA REGISTRATION	Both sides of fuselage	12 inch high letters and numbers	17038
J	Propeller Tips		4 inches from tip	33538

T-41 AIRCRAFT EXTERIOR FINISHING SYSTEM (SEE NOTE 2, PAGE 42)

Area	FORMER SYSTEM		STANDARD SYSTEM	
	Color No.	System	Color No.	System
All exterior areas except as specified			17875	MIL-C-83286
Battery Compartment			17875	MIL-C-83286
Landing Gear				
Wheel Wells			17875	MIL-C-83286
Flap Wells				
Radome				
Relief Tube Areas				
Walkways				
Engine Exhaust Path				
White Caps as Required				
Lower Fuselage				
APU Exhaust Paths				
Heater Exhaust Path				
Plastic Parts				

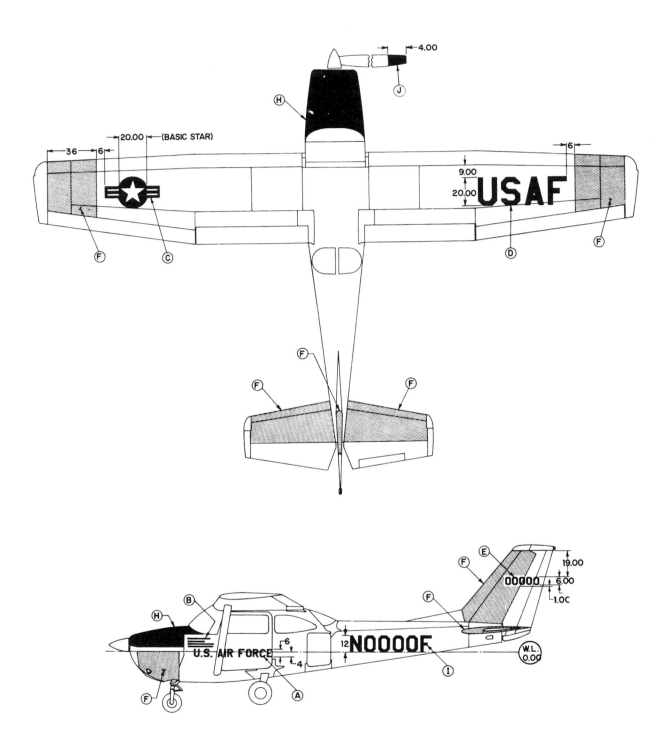

Figure B-19. T-41 Aircraft Marking Specification

T-43A AIRCRAFT MARKING SPECIFICATION (SEE FIG B-20)

1. MARKING	2. LOCATION	3. SIZE	4. COLOR NO/CODE
A U.S. AIR FORCE	Both sides of fuselage	Letters 30 inch high	15044
B Model Designation, Acft S/N and fuel Requirement	Left side of fuselage	Letters and numbers 1 inch high.	17038
C National Star	Both sides of fuselage centered 36" below center line of rear two windows	40 inch star	
D	On under surface of right wing and top surface of left wing	40 inch star	Background border - 15044, Stars and Bars - 17875, Stripes - 11136
E USAF	Top surface of right wing and under surface of left letters	30 inch high	15044
F Call Numbers	Both sides of vertical stabilizer	12 inch high numbers	17038
G Anti-Glare	Top of fuselage in front of cockpit wrapping around to station 179		37038
H Band	Both sides of fuselage through centerline of windows	20 inch wide to tapered tail	15044

T-43A AIRCRAFT EXTERIOR FINISHING SYSTEM (SEE NOTE 2, PAGE 42)

Area	FORMER SYSTEM Color No.	System	STANDARD SYSTEM Color No.	System
All exterior areas except as specified			17875	MIL-C-83286
Battery Compartment			17875	MIL-C-83286
Landing Gear				MIL-C-83286
Wheel Wells			17875	MIL-C-83286
Flap Wells			17875	MIL-C 83236
Radome			17038	MIL-C-83231, Type II
Relief Tube Areas			17875	MIL-C-83286
Walkways				
Engine Exhaust Path				
APU Exhaust Paths			17875	MIL-C-83286
Heater Exhaust Path			17875	MIL-C-83286
Plastic Parts			17038	MIL-C-83231, Type II

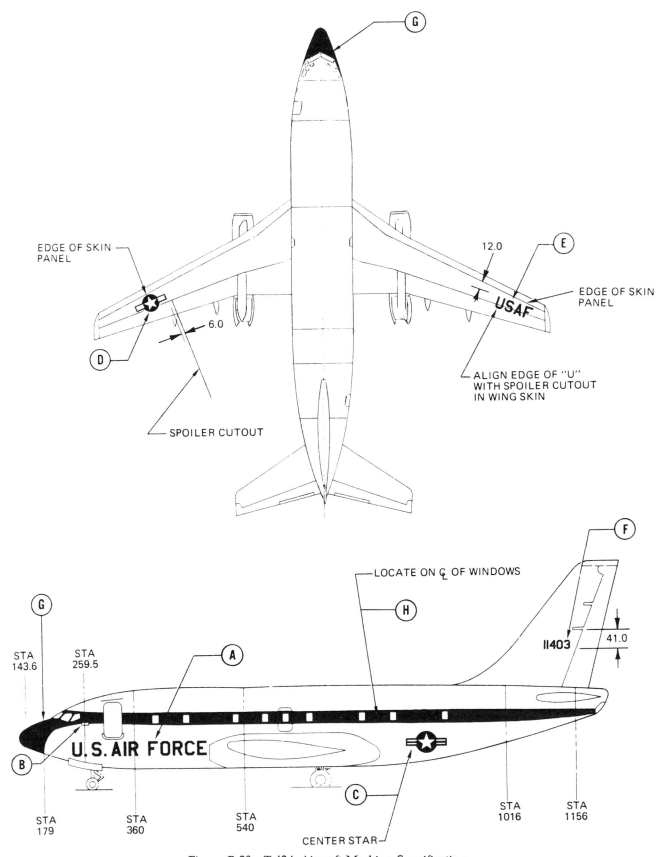

Figure B-20. T-43A Aircraft Marking Specification

SPECIAL PURPOSE AIRCRAFT MARKINGS

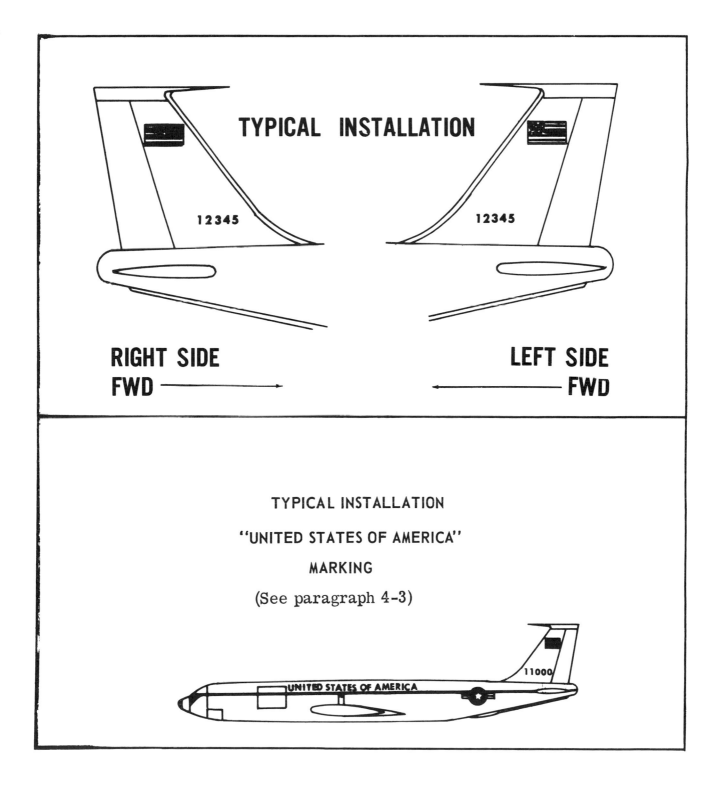

TYPICAL INSTALLATION

12345   12345

RIGHT SIDE   **LEFT SIDE**
FWD ⟶   ⟵ **FWD**

TYPICAL INSTALLATION

"UNITED STATES OF AMERICA"

MARKING

(See paragraph 4-3)

UNITED STATES OF AMERICA   11000

Figure C-1. U. S. Flag Marking

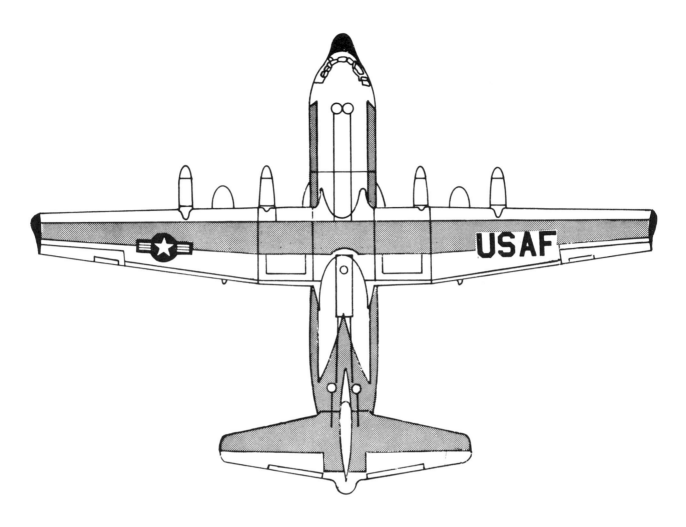

NOTE: USAF standard gray with solar resistant white cap with Insignia Red conspicuity marking 11136 and 1 inch blue border 15044. Upper and lower wing and tail surfaces are painted the same configuration.

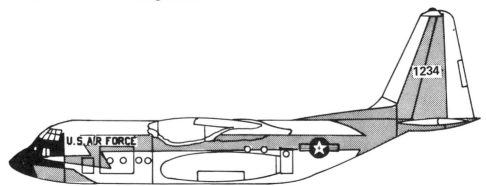

Figure C-2. RC-130 Aircraft Conspicuity Marking

[Use of these red "lightning bolt" markings fell out of fashion in the late 1970s, though Air Force tech orders continue to include drawings for C-130s, (shown here) C-140s, and T-39s.]

APPENDIX D

SPECIFICATIONS - CAMOUFLAGE PATTERNS

AND MARKINGS FOR USAF AIRCRAFT

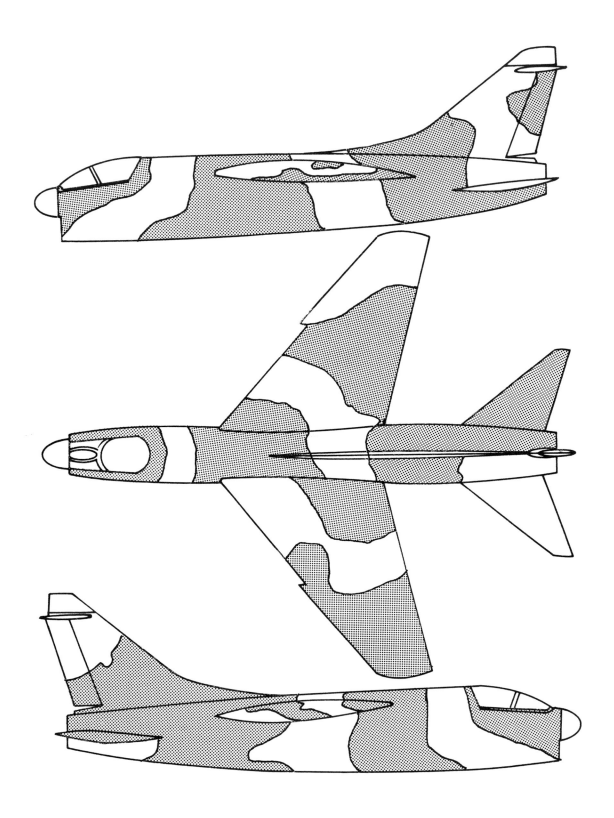

Figure D-1. ANG A-7 Aircraft Camouflage Pattern (Sheet 1 of 2)

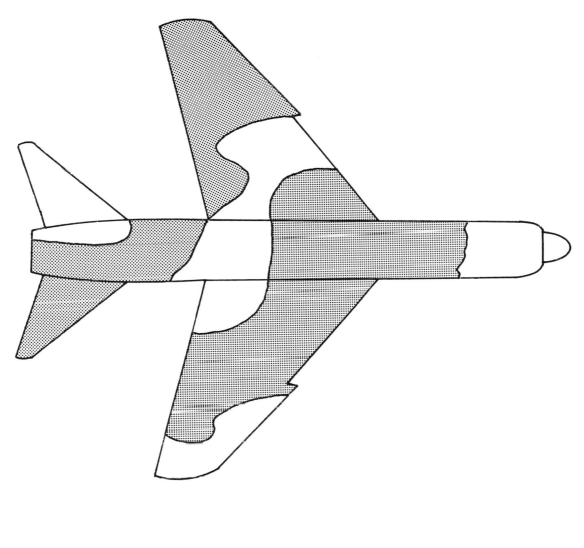

	[European Scheme]	[Gray Scheme]
	GREEN No. 34079	GRAY No. 26270
	GRAY No. 36081	GRAY No. 26118
Radome Coating:	BLACK	GRAY No. 26118

Figure D-1. ANG A-7 Aircraft Camouflage Pattern (Sheet 2 of 2)

[All USAF A-7s are assigned to the Air National Guard, which will retire the type by 1994. The all-gray scheme is rapidly replacing the "European-style" green and gray.]

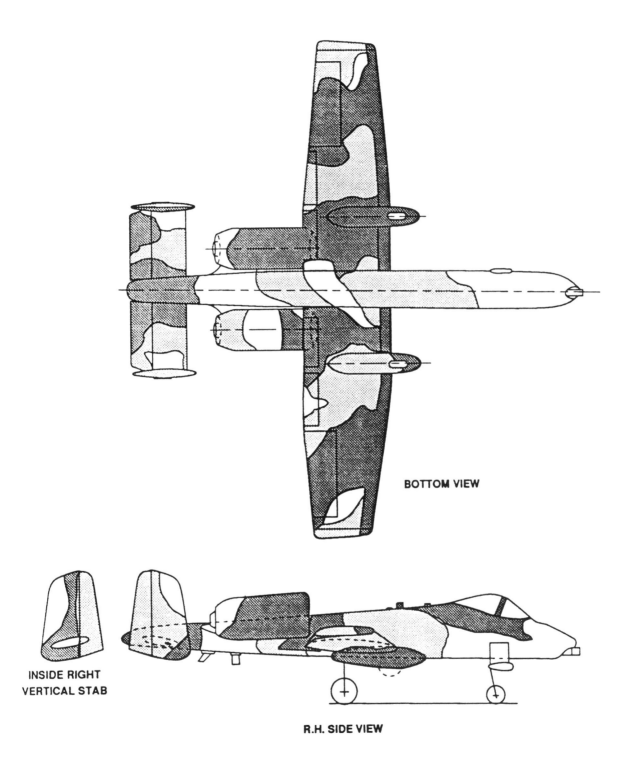

BOTTOM VIEW

**INSIDE RIGHT
VERTICAL STAB**

R.H. SIDE VIEW

Figure D-2. A-10 Aircraft Camouflage Pattern "European I" (Sheet 1 of 2)

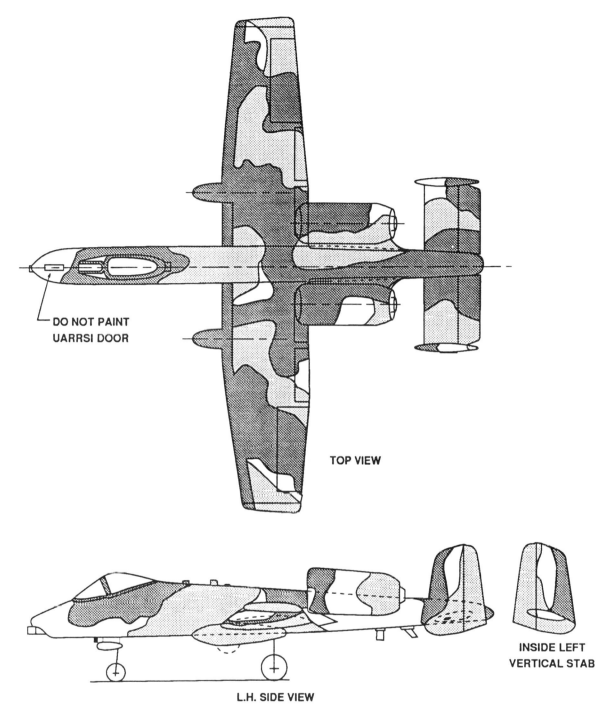

TOP VIEW

DO NOT PAINT
UARRSI DOOR

**INSIDE LEFT
VERTICAL STAB**

L.H. SIDE VIEW

APPLICATION KEY

☐ COLOR NO. 36081 DARK GRAY (GUNSHIP QUALITY)

▨ COLOR NO. 34102 LIGHT GREEN (GUNSHIP QUALITY)

▨ COLOR NO. 34092 DARK GREEN (GUNSHIP QUALITY)

NOTE

GUNSHIP QUALITY BLACK, COLOR NO. 37038
MIL-C-83286, IS USED FOR ALL INSIGNIA AND
MARKINGS. BOTH RUDDERS SHALL BE
COMPLETELY PAINTED COLOR NO. 34102
LIGHT GREEN (GUNSHIP QUALITY) WITH NO
OVERSPRAY OF OTHER COLORS.

Figure D-2. A-10 Aircraft European I Camouflage Pattern (Sheet 2 of 2)

[PACAF OA-10 Forward Air Controllers are being painted overall Gunship Gray, color number 36118.]

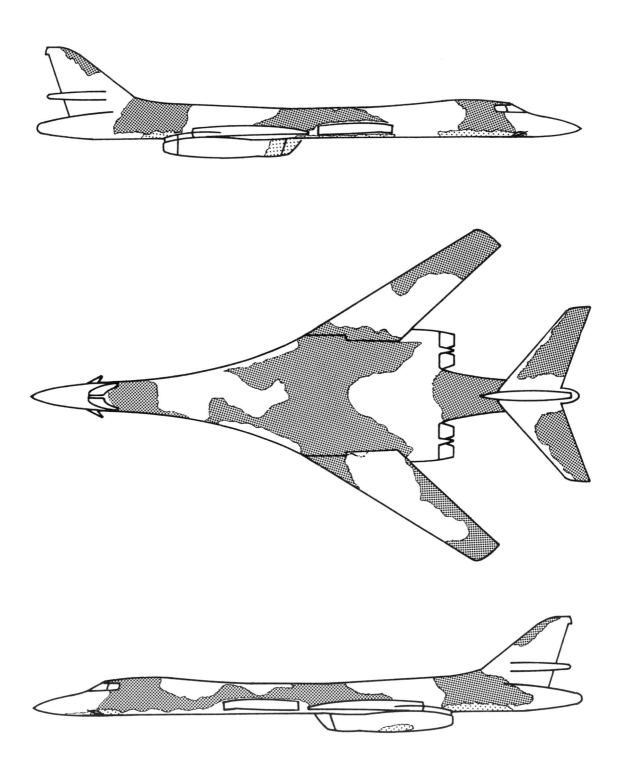

[Figure D-3. B-1B Strategic Camouflage Scheme (Sheet 1 of 2)]

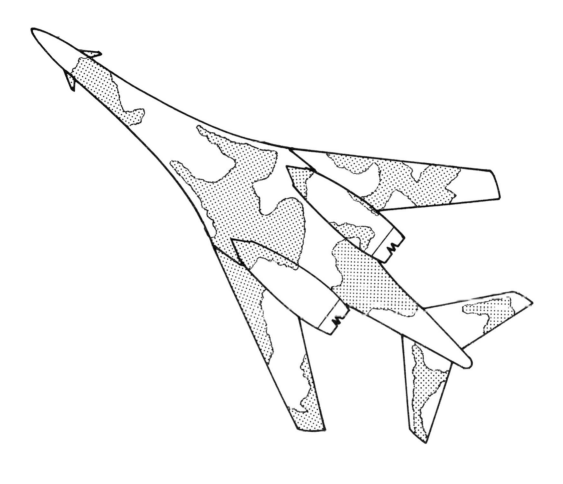

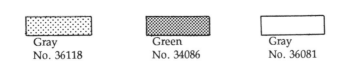

| Gray | Green | Gray |
| No. 36118 | No. 34086 | No. 36081 |

[Figure D-3. B-1B Strategic Camouflage Scheme (Sheet 2 of 2)]

[During the summer of 1991 SAC began repainting its B-1s overall gray No. 36118.]

| White No. 17875 | Tan No. 34201 | Green No. 34159 | Green No. 34079 | Gray No. 36081 |

Figure D-4. B-52 Aircraft Camouflage Pattern

[The basic scheme of this camouflage pattern dates back to the mid-1960s. In the late 1980s SAC began implementing the Strategic Camouflage Pattern (see Figure D-5). In the interim, the noses of all B-52s awaiting the new camouflage were repainted dark gray 36081. By 1990 white noses had been eliminated from the fleet.

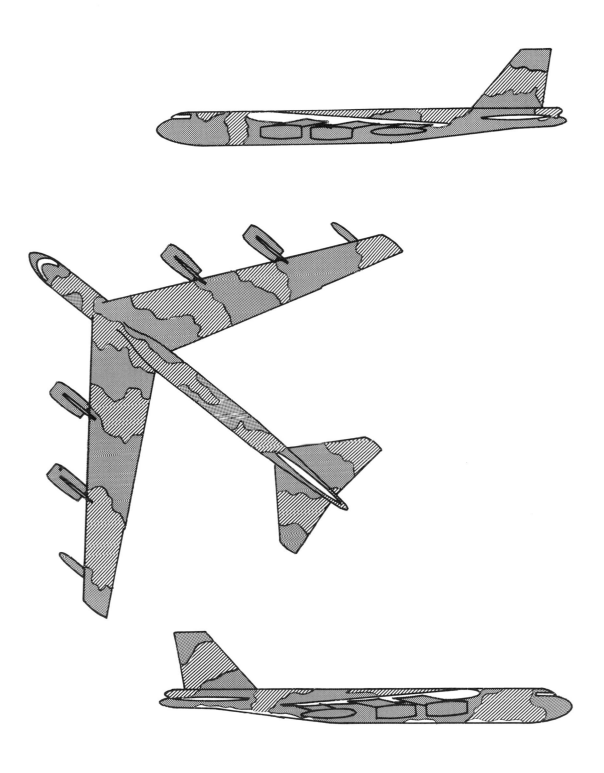

[Figure D-5. B-52 Strategic Camouflage Scheme (Sheet 1 of 2)]

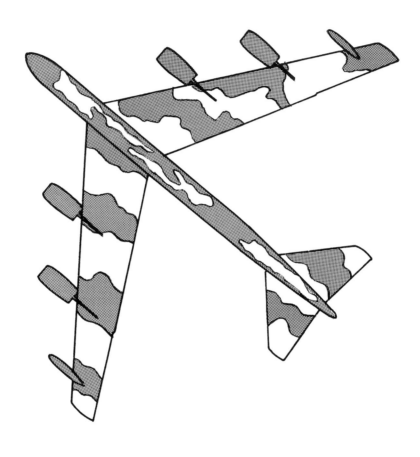

| Gray | Green | Gray |
| No. 36118 | No. 34086 | No. 36081 |

[Figure D-5. B-52 Strategic Camouflage Scheme (Sheet 2 of 2)]

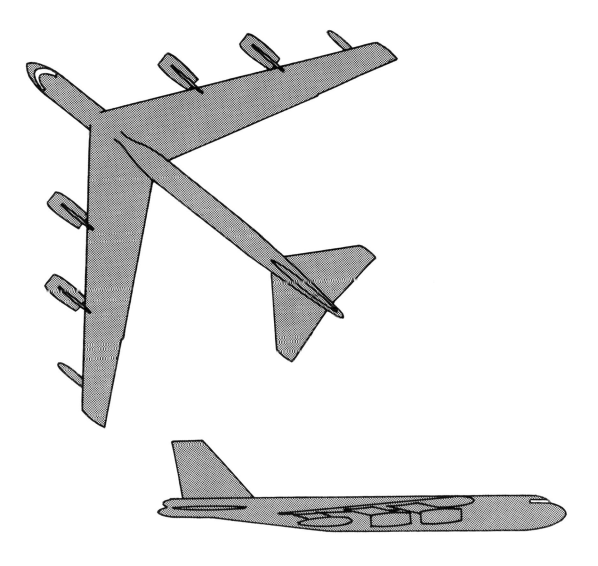

[Figure D-6. B-52 Monochromatic Camouflage Scheme]

[During 1988 SAC abandoned the Strategic Camouflage Scheme for B-52s (Figure D-5), switching instead to overall gray No. 36081. Late in 1990 the scheme was modified, with gray No. 36118 replacing the darker gray No. 36081. At this writing it is possible to find B-52s in any of the four schemes described here.]

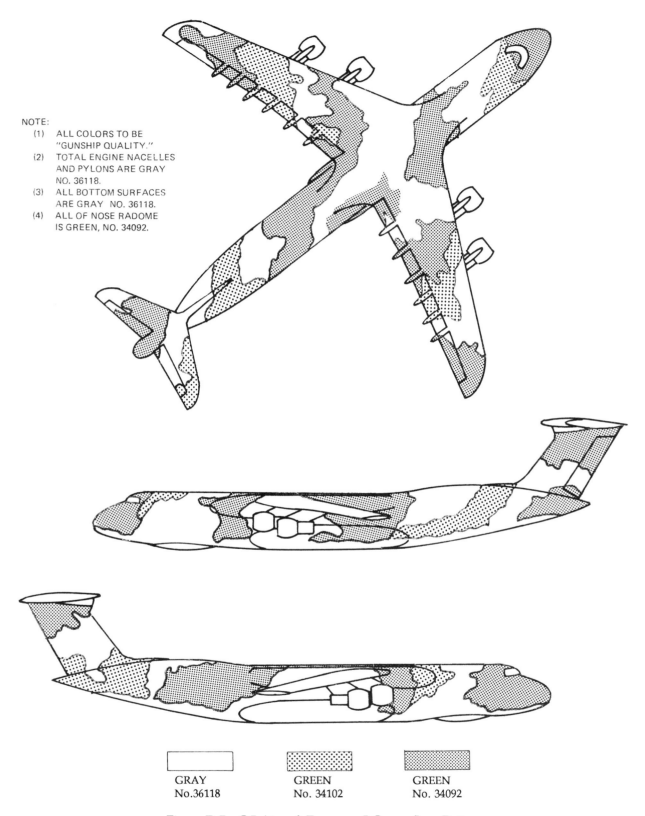

NOTE:
(1) ALL COLORS TO BE "GUNSHIP QUALITY."
(2) TOTAL ENGINE NACELLES AND PYLONS ARE GRAY NO. 36118.
(3) ALL BOTTOM SURFACES ARE GRAY NO. 36118.
(4) ALL OF NOSE RADOME IS GREEN, NO. 34092.

GRAY
No.36118

GREEN
No. 34102

GREEN
No. 34092

Figure D-7. C-5 Aircraft European I Camouflage Pattern.

[In September 1991 MAC announced plans to repaint its C-5 fleet an overall gray. The color "Battle Gray" is currently planned, either in flat color number 16173 or semi-gloss 26173.]

	Gray		Dark Gray
	No. 16473		No. 36081

[Figure D-8. KC-10A Aircraft Camouflage Pattern.]

[Crews call this KC-10 color scheme "Shamu" (after the killer whale). Also, several KC-10s are painted gray No. 16473 with white tops. In August 1991 SAC announced plans to repaint its tanker fleet in overall Dark Ghost Gray No. 36320.]

NOTE:
(1) ALL COLORS TO BE "GUNSHIP" QUALITY.
(2) EXTERNAL FUEL TANKS ALL GRAY NO. 36118.
(3) TOTAL ENGINE NACELLES ARE ALL GREEN NO. 34092.
(4) BOTTOM SURFACES ARE GRAY NO. 36118.

GRAY No.36118	GREEN No. 34102	GREEN No. 34092

Figure D-9. C-130 Aircraft European I Camouflage Pattern.

[During the summer of 1991 MAC evaluated a single C-130 painted in overall "Battle Gray," color number 36173. In September 1991 MAC announced plans to repaint the entire C-130 fleet in that color or semi-gloss 26173. Although most AFSOC AC-130s are painted overall Gunship Gray, color number 36118, at least one new AC-130U has been delivered in European I.]

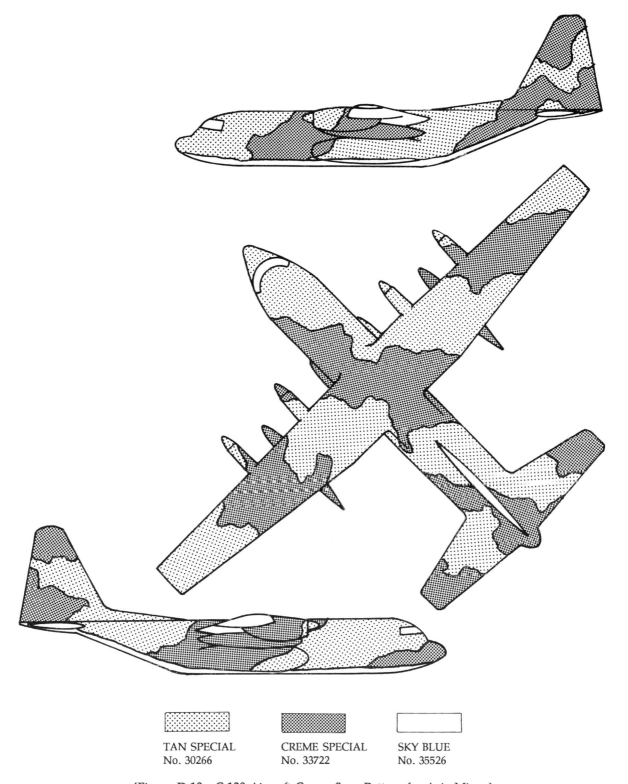

| TAN SPECIAL | CREME SPECIAL | SKY BLUE |
| No. 30266 | No. 33722 | No. 35526 |

[Figure D-10. C-130 Aircraft Camouflage Pattern for Asia Minor]

[During 1981 MAC initiated a program to repaint 40 regular Air Force C-130s in this scheme as a contingency for operations the Middle East or Northern Africa. Despite the drawings on this page, most aircraft had nacelles and undersides of wings and tail painted Creme Special. Crews disliked the scheme, which was soon discontinued, but a few aircraft could still be found in these colors in 1990.]

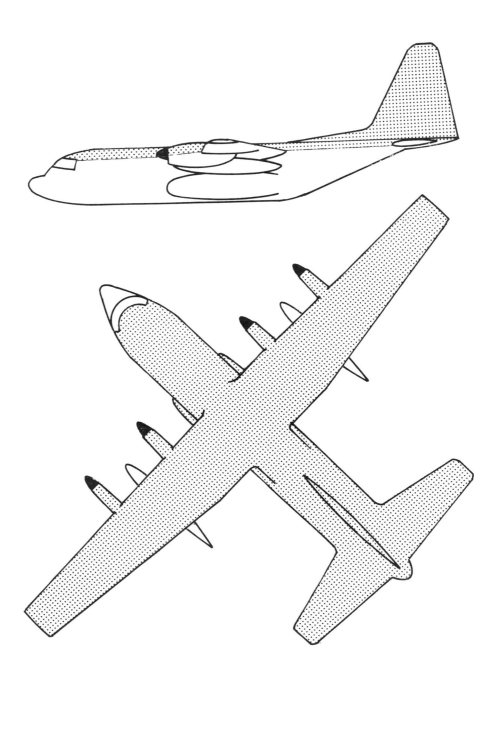

	Gray No. 36492		Compass Ghost Gray No. 36320

[Figure D-11. EC-130 Aircraft Camouflage Pattern.]

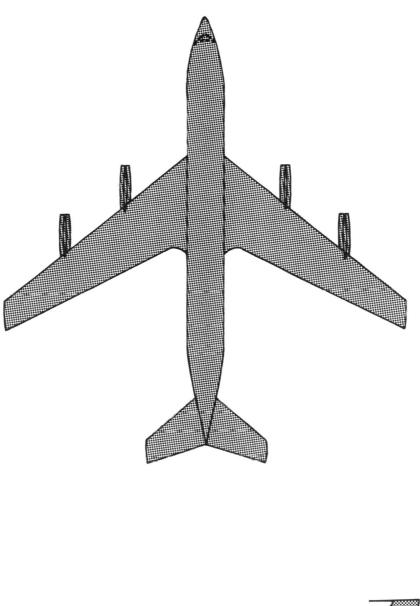

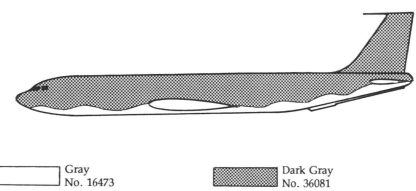

Gray
No. 16473

Dark Gray
No. 36081

[Figure D-12. KC-135 Aircraft Camouflage Pattern.]

[Crews call this KC-135 color scheme "Baby Shamu" (a smaller version of the KC-10 scheme). The scheme has also been applied
to E-8 J-STARS aircraft. In August 1991 SAC announced plans to repaint its tanker fleet in overall Dark Ghost Gray No. 36320.]

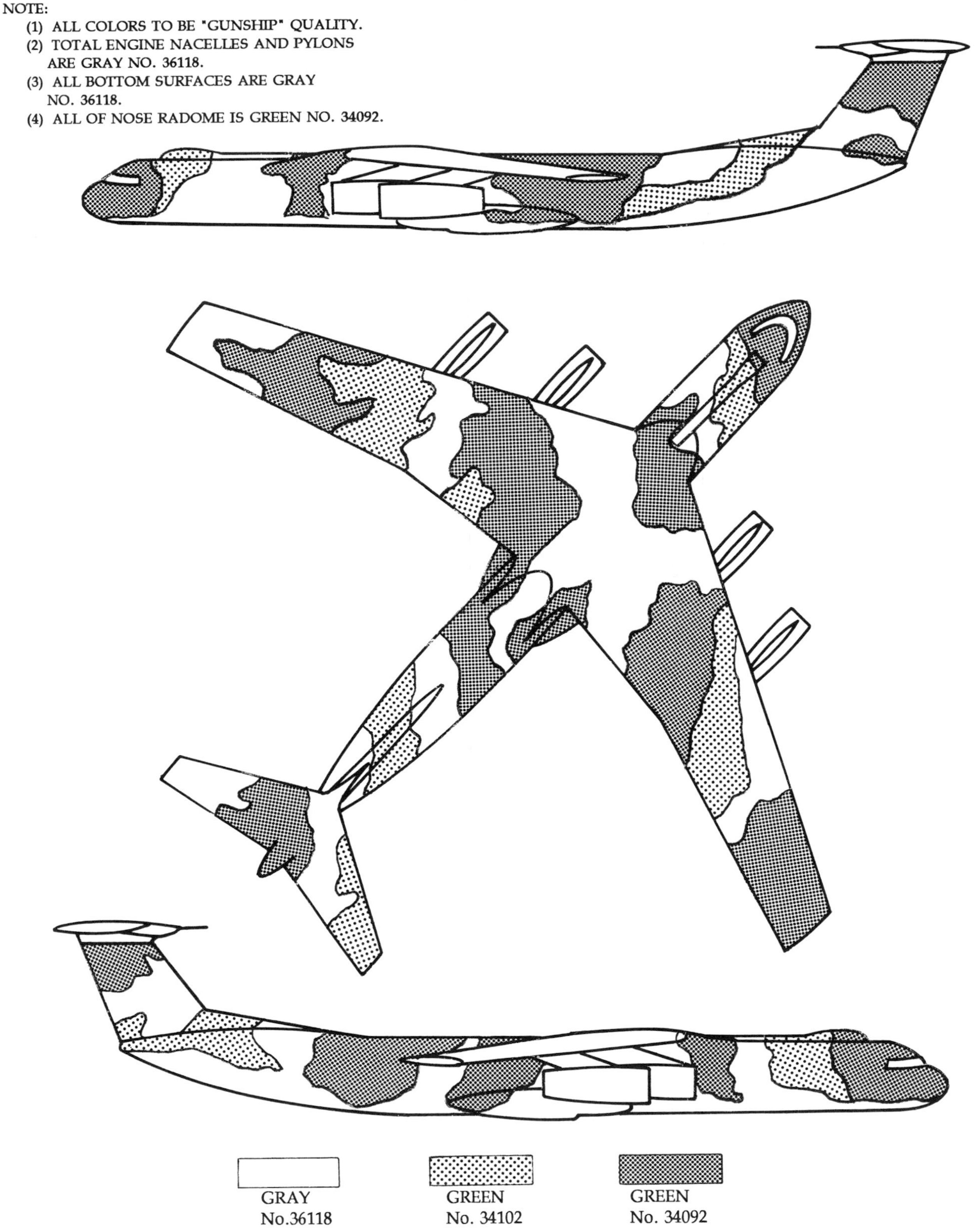

NOTE:
  (1) ALL COLORS TO BE "GUNSHIP" QUALITY.
  (2) TOTAL ENGINE NACELLES AND PYLONS
      ARE GRAY NO. 36118.
  (3) ALL BOTTOM SURFACES ARE GRAY
      NO. 36118.
  (4) ALL OF NOSE RADOME IS GREEN NO. 34092.

GRAY	GREEN	GREEN
No.36118	No. 34102	No. 34092

Figure D-13. C-141B Aircraft Camoulage Pattern, European I

[In September 1991 MAC announced plans to repaint its C-141 fleet an overall gray. The color "Battle Gray" is currently planned, either in flat color number 16173 or semi-gloss 26173.]

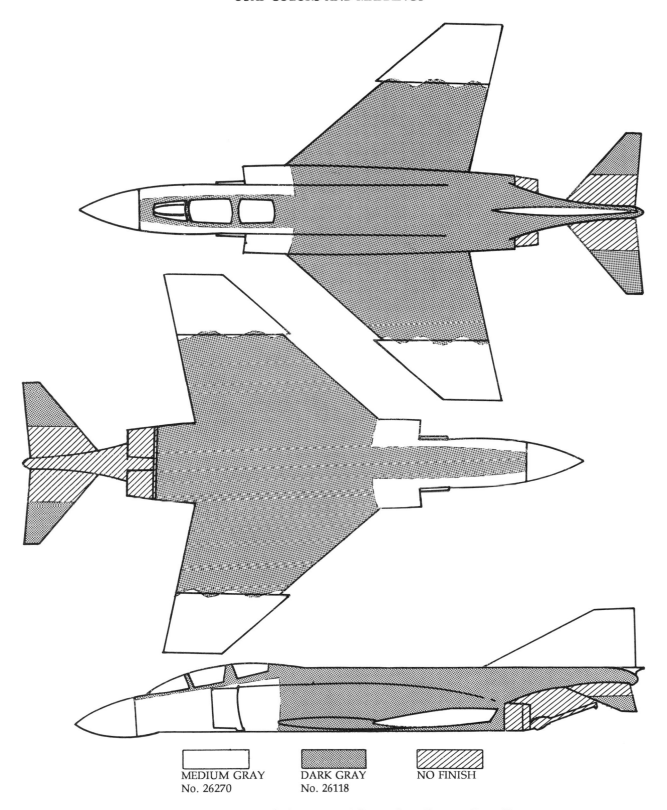

MEDIUM GRAY
No. 26270

DARK GRAY
No. 26118

NO FINISH

Figure D-14. F/RF-4 Aircraft Wraparound Camouflage Exterior Paint Pattern

[This scheme originated as the Project Hill Camouflage Scheme, a graded pattern using the same colors as the F-16. Input from the field created this two-toned wrap-around variation, known as Hill Gray II. The original Project Hill scheme was redesignated Hill Gray I and abandoned (although several Hill Gray I F-4s could still be found in 1990).

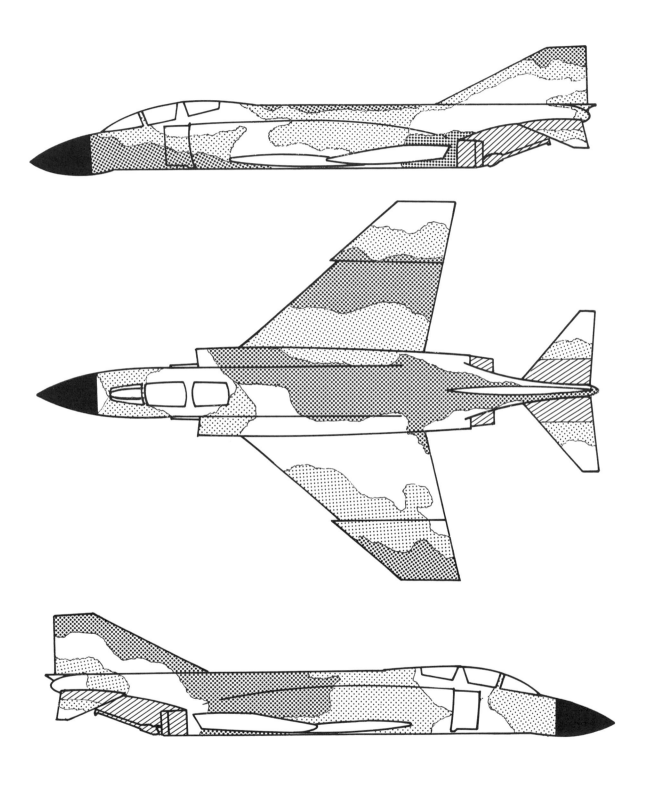

[Figure D-15. F/RF-4 Aircraft Wraparound Camouflage Exterior Paint Pattern (Sheet 1 of 2)]

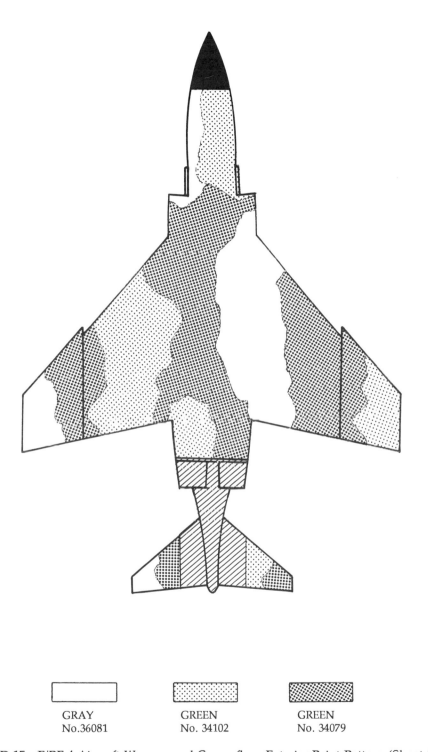

GRAY
No.36081

GREEN
No. 34102

GREEN
No. 34079

[Figure D-15. F/RF-4 Aircraft Wraparound Camouflage Exterior Paint Pattern (Sheet 2 of 2)]

[The F-4's unique version of "European I" (note the substitution of 34079 for the standard 34092) is no longer included in TO 1-1-4. A very small number of F-4Es still wear this pattern; all be retired or repainted during 1992.

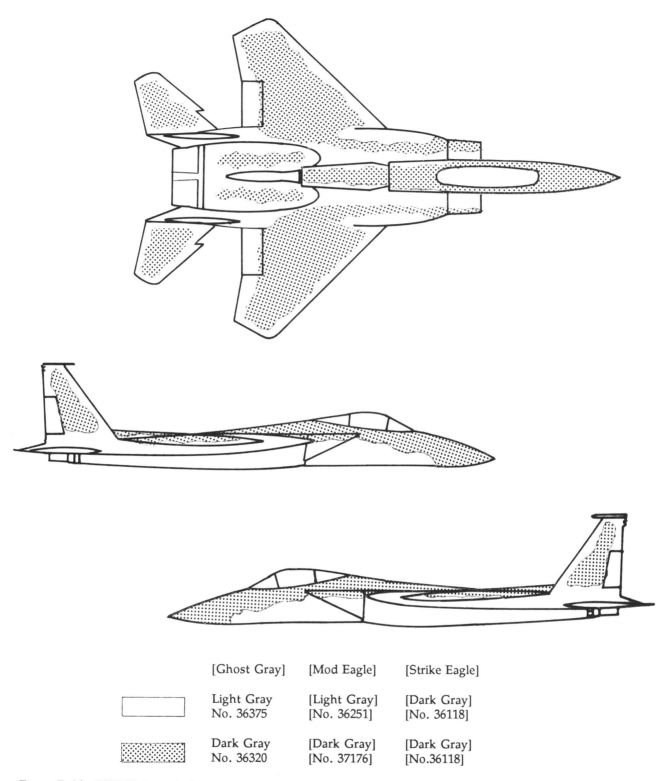

	[Ghost Gray]	[Mod Eagle]	[Strike Eagle]
	Light Gray No. 36375	[Light Gray] [No. 36251]	[Dark Gray] [No. 36118]
	Dark Gray No. 36320	[Dark Gray] [No. 37176]	[Dark Gray] [No.36118]

Figure D-16. F/TF-15 Aircraft Camouflage Pattern for High and Low Reflectance Gray

[F-15As, Bs, Cs, and Ds now use distinct camouflages: the original TAC Ghost Gray scheme and PACAF's higher contrast Mod Eagle scheme. (The PACAF colors are applied only to the 21st TFW in Alaska, the 18th TFW in Japan, and the Hawaiian ANG's 154th Composite Group.) All F-15Es are painted overall Gunship Gray, color number 36118. All 'TF-15's were redesignated as F-15Bs in the mid-1970s.]

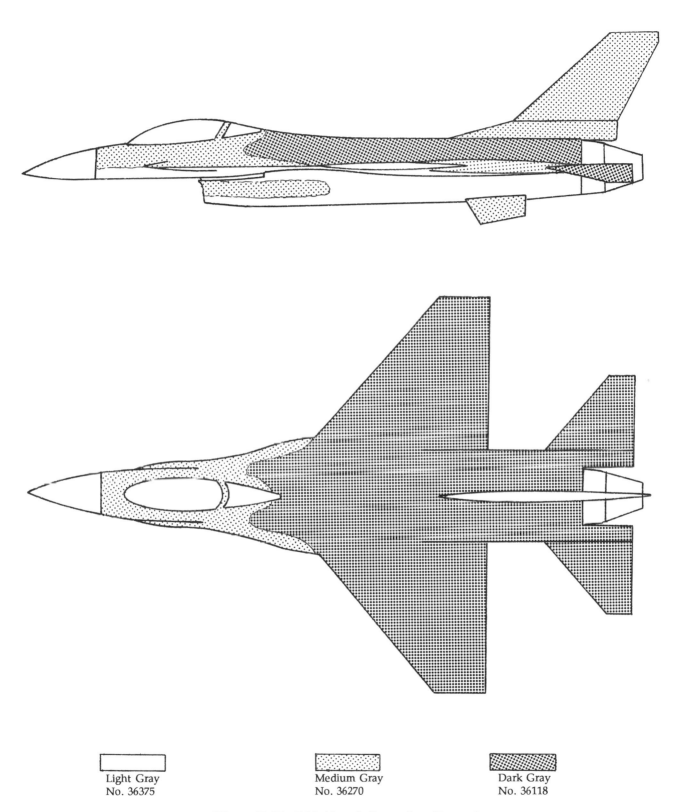

Light Gray
No. 36375

Medium Gray
No. 36270

Dark Gray
No. 36118

[Figure D-17. F-16 Aircraft Camouflage Pattern]

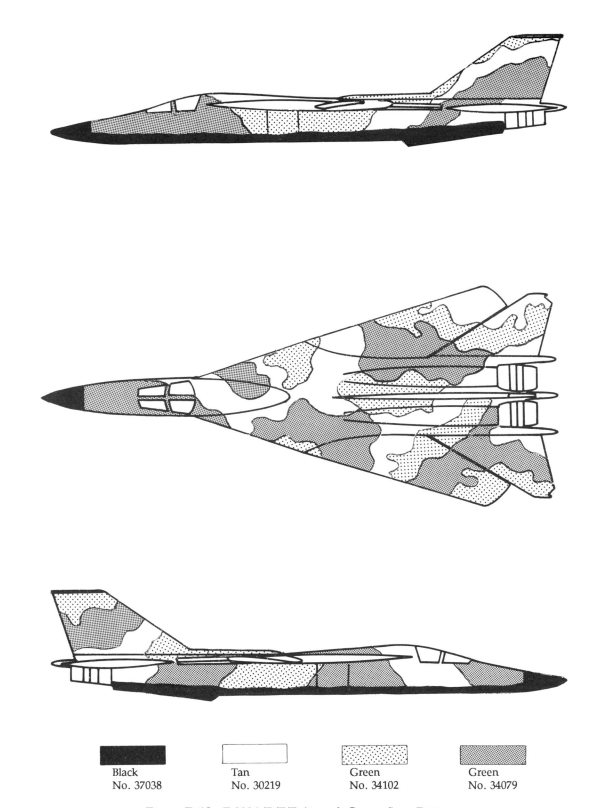

| Black No. 37038 | Tan No. 30219 | Green No. 34102 | Green No. 34079 |

Figure D-18. F-111A/D/E/F Aircraft Camouflage Pattern

[Although tech orders specify flat black No. 37038, gloss black No. 17038 is used exclusively. Since 1990 the tactical fleet of F-111s - which includes all FB-111As converted to F-111Gs - has been converting to a color scheme of overall gray No. 36118.]

NOTE

Pylons and bottoms of fuel tanks will be
painted iaw TO 1F-111(B)A-2-1-1.

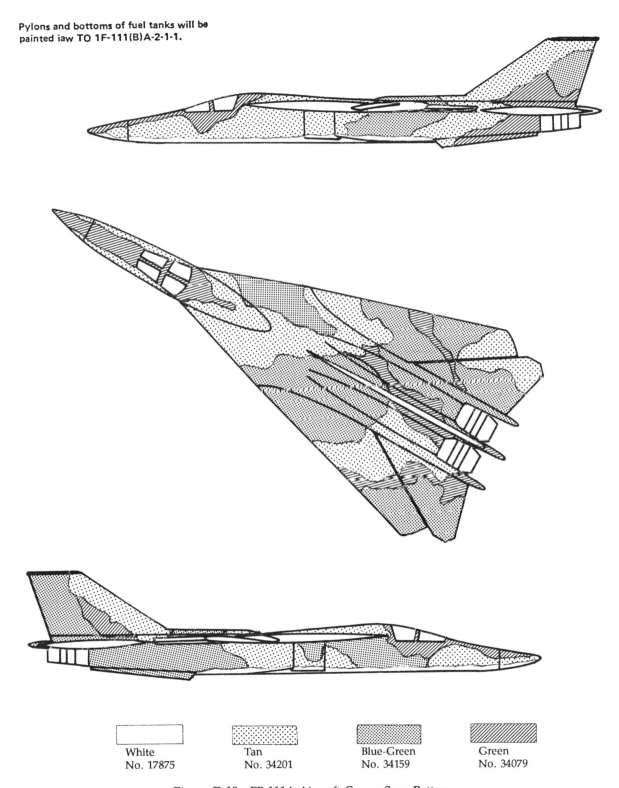

White	Tan	Blue-Green	Green
No. 17875	No. 34201	No. 34159	No. 34079

Figure D-19. FB-111A Aircraft Camouflage Pattern

[SAC dropped the FB-111A from inventory during 1990/91. Many have been transferred to TAC as F-111Gs (see Figure D-18).

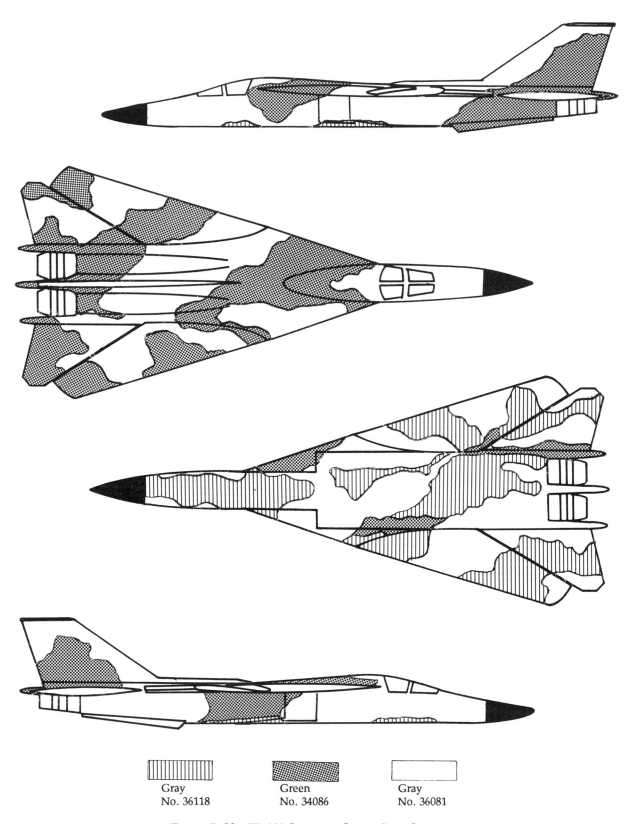

Gray
No. 36118

Green
No. 34086

Gray
No. 36081

Figure D-20. FB-111 Strategic Camouflage Scheme

[111s are called "Aardvarks" by their crews; FB-111s in the Strategic Camouflage Scheme were called "Dark Varks."]

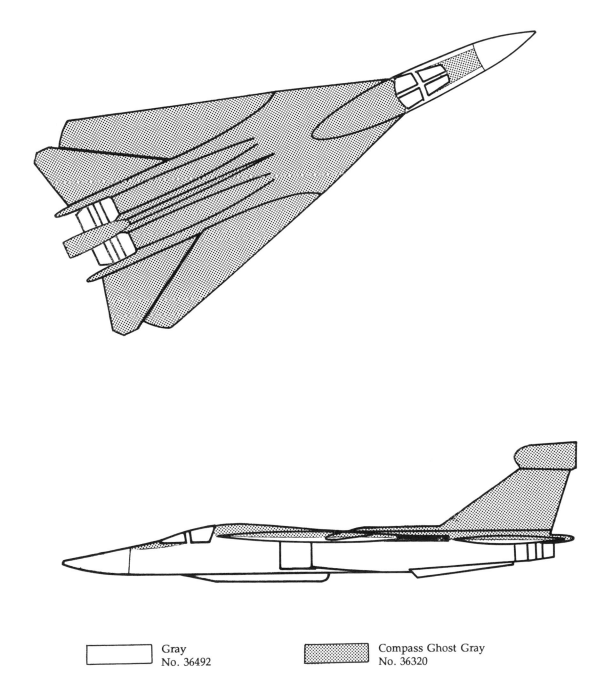

	Gray		Compass Ghost Gray
	No. 36492		No. 36320

[Figure D-21. EF-111 Aircraft Camouflage Pattern.]

[The electonic warfare EF-111 - "Spark Varks" to the crews - originally used grayish blue No. 35237 for the antiglare panel.]

MAIN AND TAIL ROTOR BLADES - FLAT BLACK, COLOR NO. 37038. PAINT AT DEPOT ONLY. FIELD MAINTENANCE PAINTING LIMITED TO TOUCH-UP REPAIR.

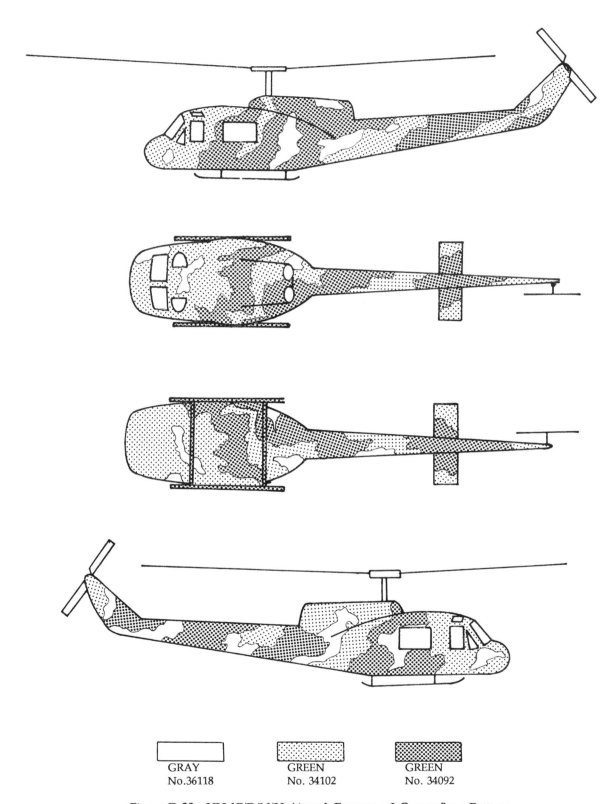

GRAY	GREEN	GREEN
No.36118	No. 34102	No. 34092

Figure D-22. UH-1F/D/N/H Aircraft European I Camouflage Pattern

MAIN AND TAIL ROTOR BLADES - FLAT BLACK, COLOR NO. 37038. PAINT AT DEPOT ONLY. FIELD MAINTENANCE PAINTING LIMITED TO TOUCH-UP REPAIR.

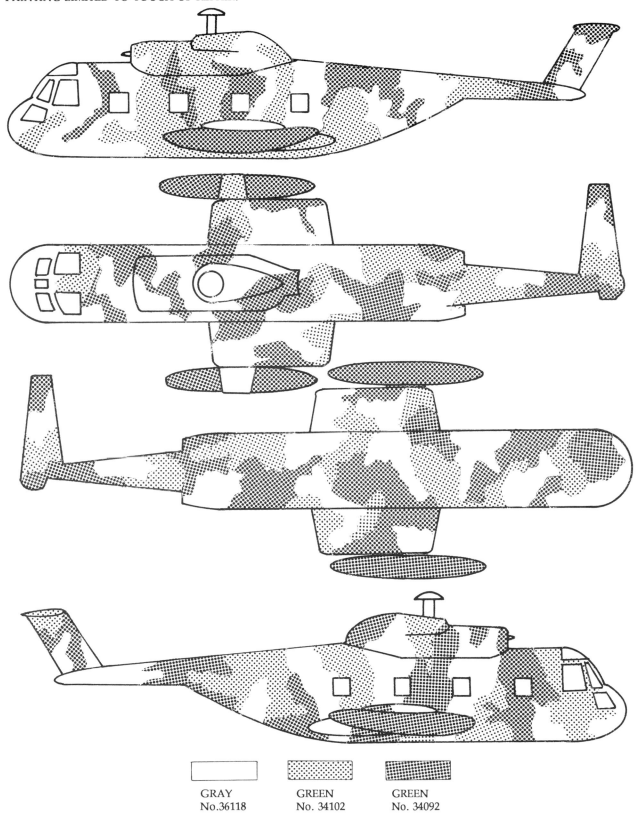

| GRAY | GREEN | GREEN |
| No.36118 | No. 34102 | No. 34092 |

Figure D-23. CH-3 [HH-3, MH-3] Aircraft European I Camouflage Pattern

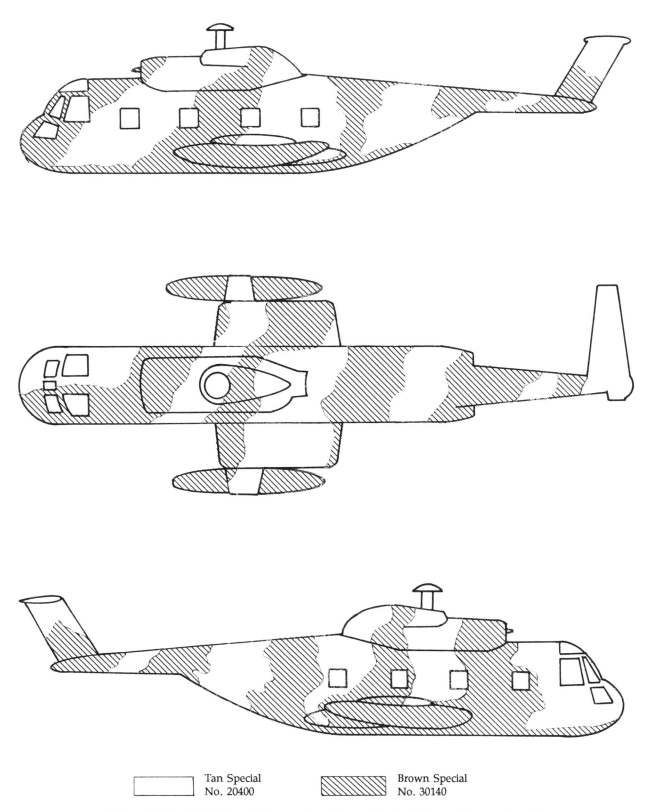

Tan Special
No. 20400

Brown Special
No. 30140

[Figure D-24. H-3 Aircraft Camouflage Pattern for Asia Minor (Desert Storm)]

[These schematics are redrafted from AFSOC drawings; photos show some aircraft used Tan, not Brown, undersurfaces.]

MAIN AND TAIL ROTOR BLADES - FLAT BLACK, COLOR NO. 37038. PAINT AT DEPOT ONLY. FIELD MAINTENANCE PAINTING LIMITED TO TOUCH-UP REPAIR. MAIN ROTOR HUB TO BE BLACK NO. 37038.

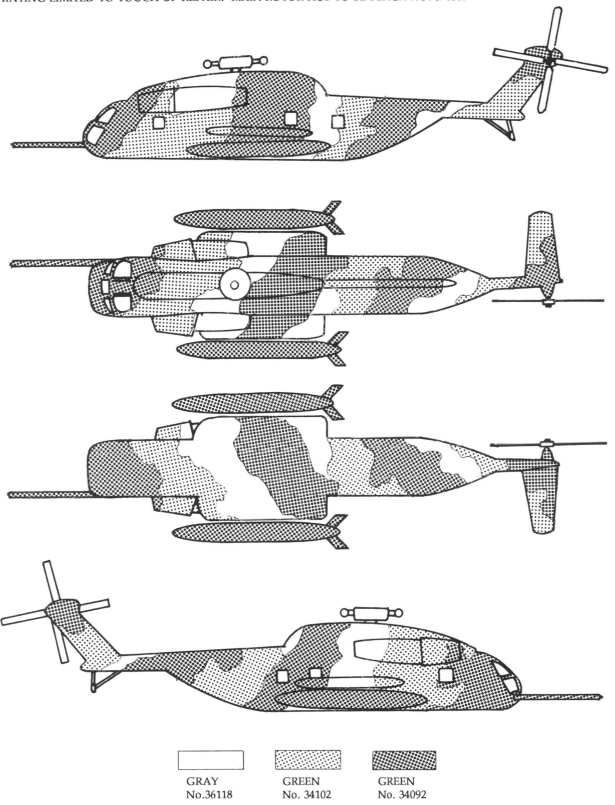

| GRAY
No.36118 | GREEN
No. 34102 | GREEN
No. 34092 |

Figure D-25. H-53 Aircraft European I Camouflage Pattern

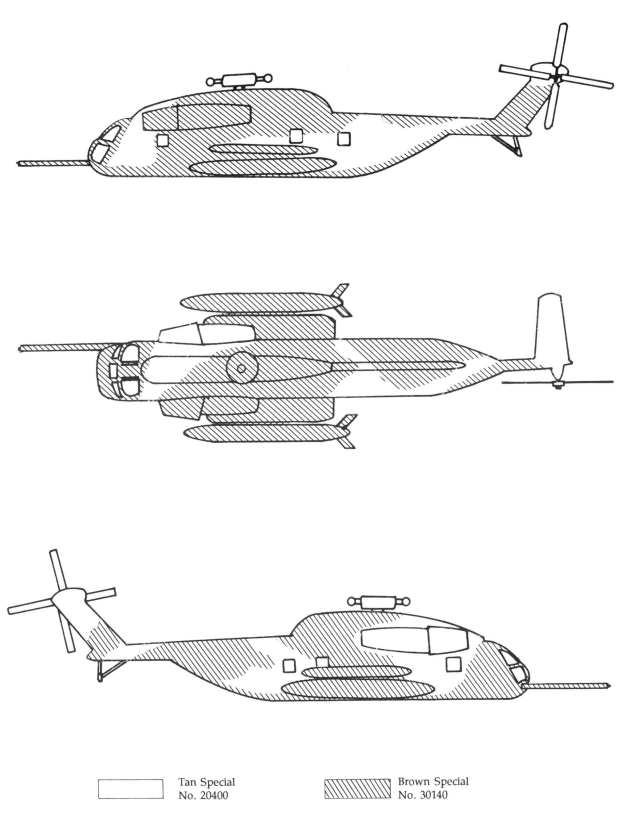

Tan Special
No. 20400

Brown Special
No. 30140

[Figure D-26. H-53 Aircraft Camouflage Pattern for Asia Minor (Desert Storm)]

[These schematics are redrafted from AFSOC drawings; photos show some aircraft used Tan, not Brown, undersurfaces.]

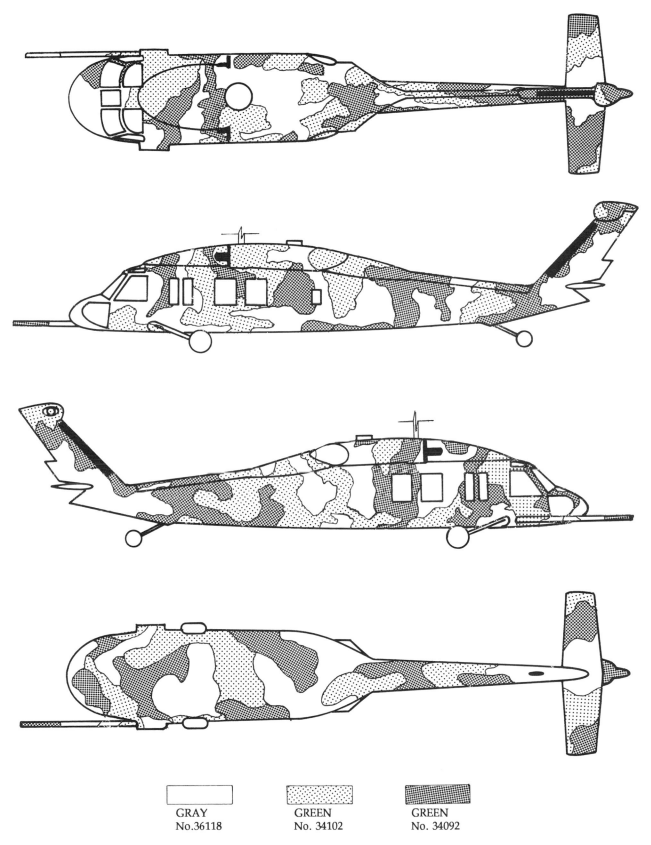

GRAY	GREEN	GREEN
No.36118	No. 34102	No. 34092

[Figure D-27. H-60 Aircraft European I Camouflage Pattern]

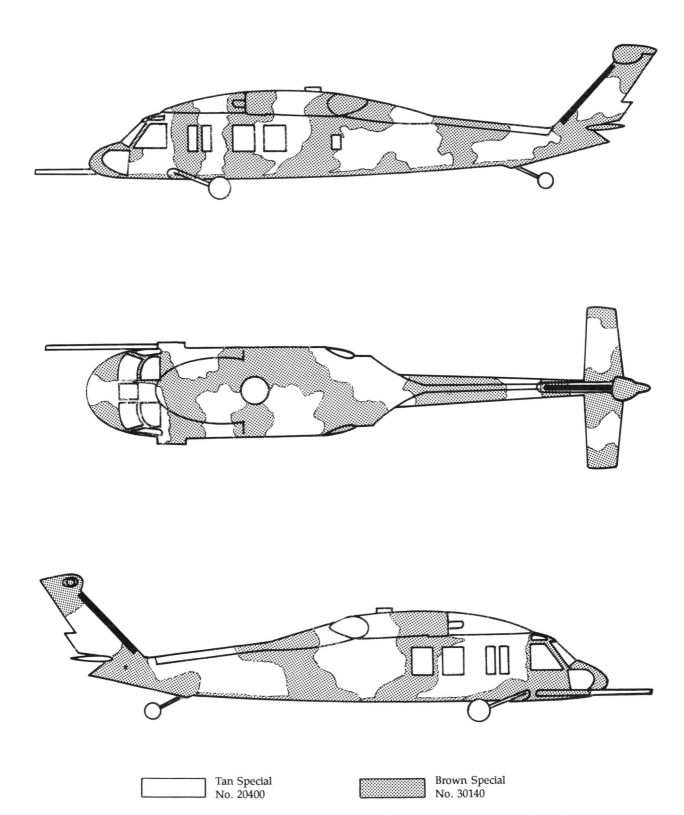

| | Tan Special No. 20400 | | Brown Special No. 30140 |

[Figure D-28. H-60 Aircraft Camouflage Pattern for Asia Minor (Desert Storm)]

[These schematics are redrafted from AFSOC drawings; photos show some aircraft used Tan, not Brown, undersurfaces.]

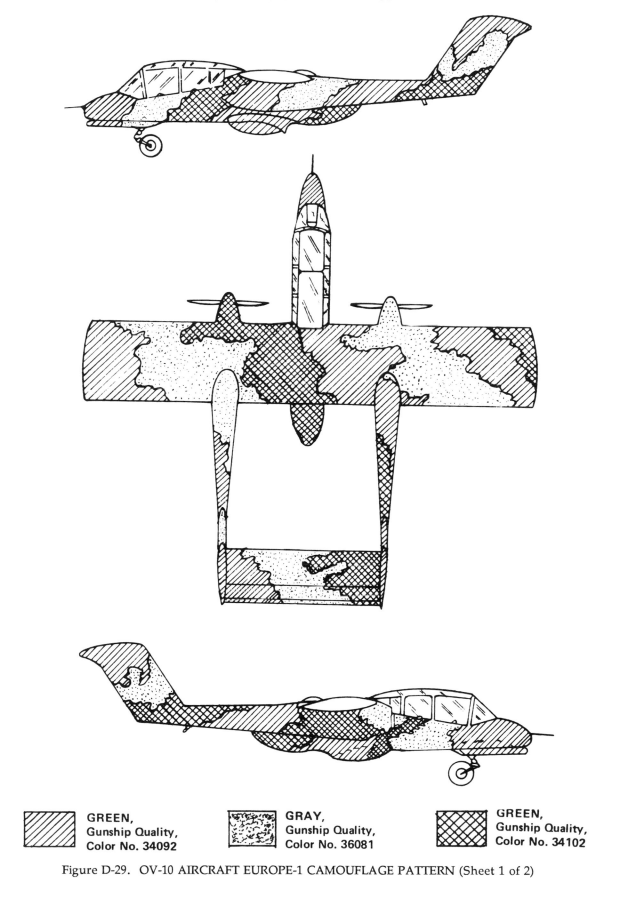

| GREEN, Gunship Quality, Color No. 34092 | GRAY, Gunship Quality, Color No. 36081 | GREEN, Gunship Quality, Color No. 34102 |

Figure D-29. OV-10 AIRCRAFT EUROPE-1 CAMOUFLAGE PATTERN (Sheet 1 of 2)

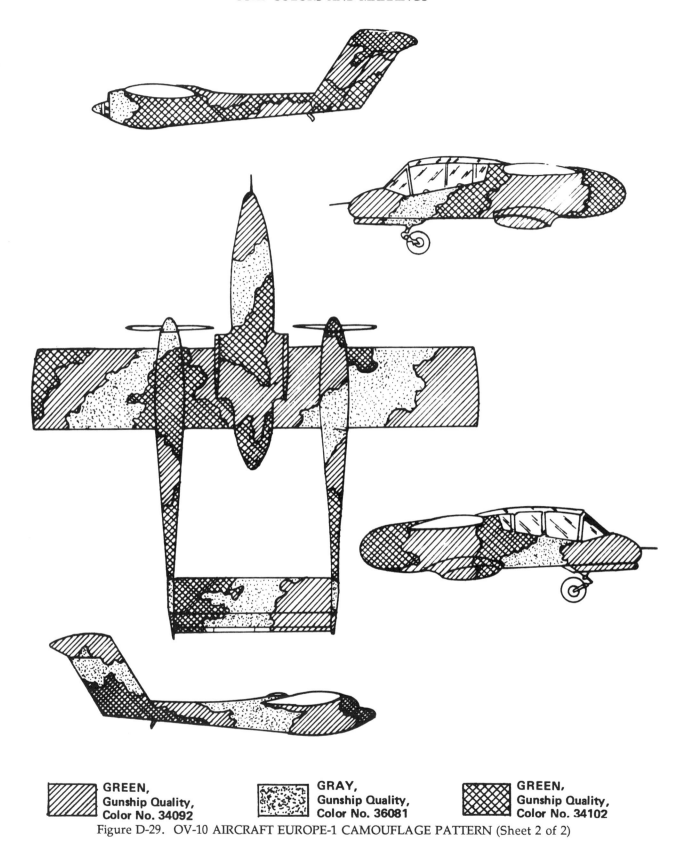

| GREEN, Gunship Quality, Color No. 34092 | GRAY, Gunship Quality, Color No. 36081 | GREEN, Gunship Quality, Color No. 34102 |

Figure D-29. OV-10 AIRCRAFT EUROPE-1 CAMOUFLAGE PATTERN (Sheet 2 of 2)

[In TO 1-1-4, the adjective "Europe-1" is used only to describe the OV-10's camouflage. All other similar camouflage patterns are described as "European I."]

TABLE D-1

DISTINCTIVE UNIT MARKINGS, SIZES, AND LOCATIONS, CAMOUFLAGED AIRCRAFT

(Figures D-30 through D-33 are standard size markings to be used.)

AIRCRAFT MODEL	FIGUREREFERENCE
TYPICAL DISTINCTIVE UNIT AIRCRAFT IDENTIFICATION MARKINGS.	D-30
TYPICAL DISTINCTIVE UNIT AIRCRAFT IDENTIFICATION, 24" LETTER SIZES.	D-31
TYPICAL DISTINCTIVE UNIT AIRCRAFT IDENTIFICATION, 36" LETTER SIZES	D-32
TYPICAL DISTINCTIVE UNIT AIRCRAFT SERIAL NUMBER, 15" SIZE	D-33
A-10	D-34
C-130	D-35
F/RF-4	D-36
F-15	D-37
F-16	D-38
UH-1	D-39

IMPORTANT

THE FOLLOWING INSTRUCTIONS FOR THE APPLICATION OF UNIT AIRCRAFT IDENTIFICATION MARKINGS ON THE VERTICAL STABILIZERS CAN VARY SLIGHTLY. IN NO INSTANCE WILL THESE MARKINGS BE APPLIED IN SUCH A LOCATION THAT WOULD INTERFERE WITH THE PERFORMANCE OF ANTENNAE OR OTHER EQUIPMENT INSTALLED ON THE EXTERIOR SURFACES OF THESE VERTICAL STABILIZERS.

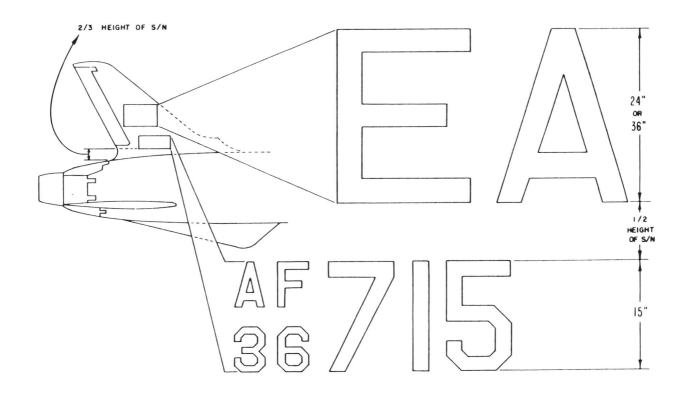

Figure D-30. TYPICAL DISTINCTIVE UNIT AIRCRAFT IDENTIFICATION MARKINGS

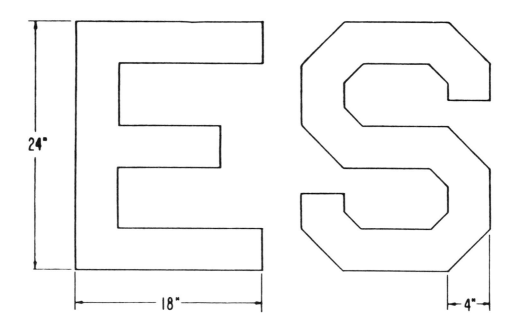

Figure D-31. TYPICAL DISTINCTIVE UNIT AIRCRAFT IDENTIFICATION, 24" LETTER SIZES

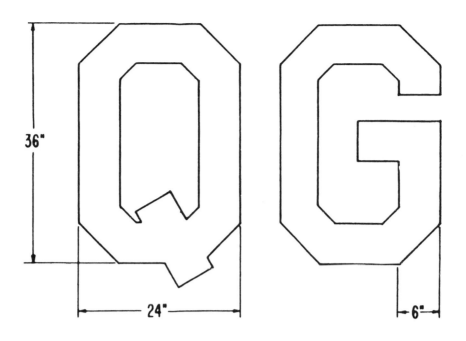

Figure D-32. TYPICAL DISTINCTIVE UNIT AIRCRAFT IDENTIFICATION, 36" LETTER SIZES

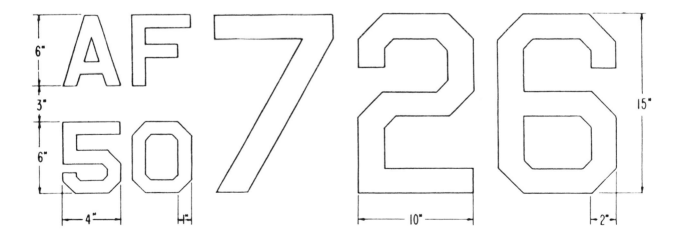

Figure D-33. TYPICAL DISTINCTIVE AIRCRAFT SERIAL NUMBER SIZES, 15" SIZE

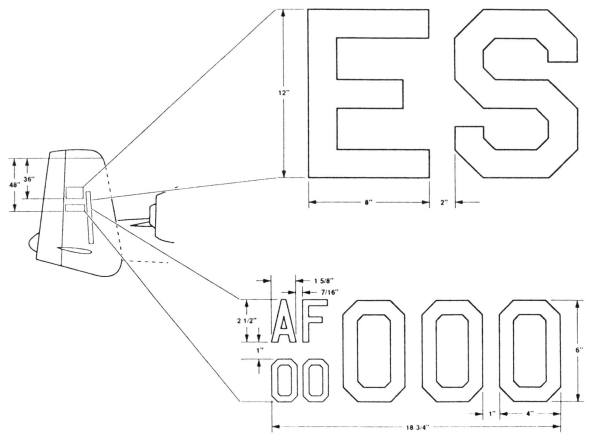

Figure D-34. DISTINCTIVE UNIT AND SERIAL NUMBER SIZES, A-10 AIRCRAFT

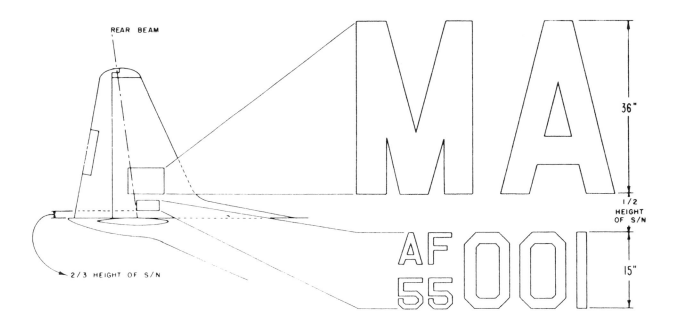

Figure D-35. DISTINCTIVE UNIT AND SERIAL NUMBER SIZES, C-130 AIRCRAFT

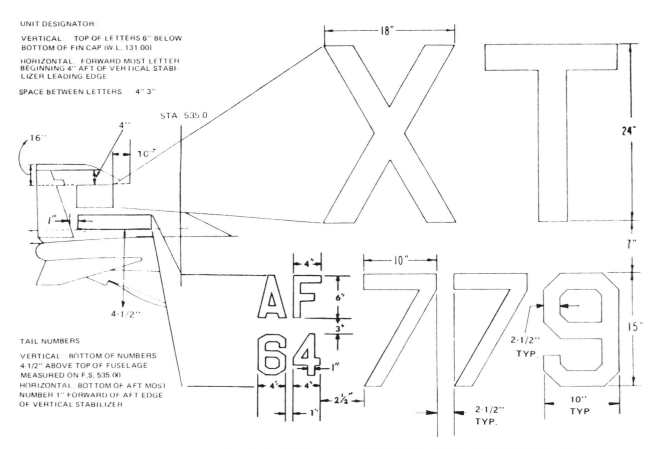

UNIT DESIGNATOR:

VERTICAL: TOP OF LETTERS 6" BELOW
BOTTOM OF FIN CAP (W.L. 131.00)

HORIZONTAL: FORWARD MOST LETTER
BEGINNING 4" AFT OF VERTICAL STABI-
LIZER LEADING EDGE

SPACE BETWEEN LETTERS 4" 3"

TAIL NUMBERS

VERTICAL: BOTTOM OF NUMBERS
4-1/2" ABOVE TOP OF FUSELAGE
MEASURED ON F.S. 535.00

HORIZONTAL: BOTTOM OF AFT MOST
NUMBER 1" FORWARD OF AFT EDGE
OF VERTICAL STABILIZER

Figure D-36. DISTINCTIVE UNIT AND SERIAL NUMBER SIZES, F/RF-4 AIRCRAFT

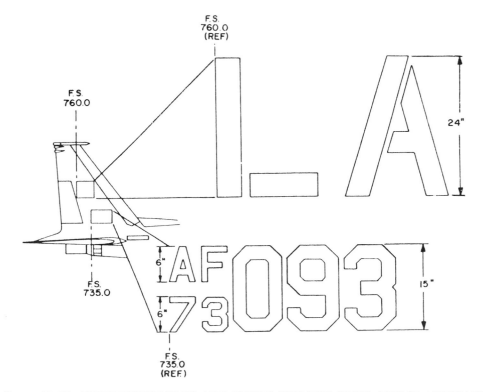

Figure D-37. DISTINCTIVE UNIT AND SERIAL NUMBER SIZES, F/TF-15 AIRCRAFT

119

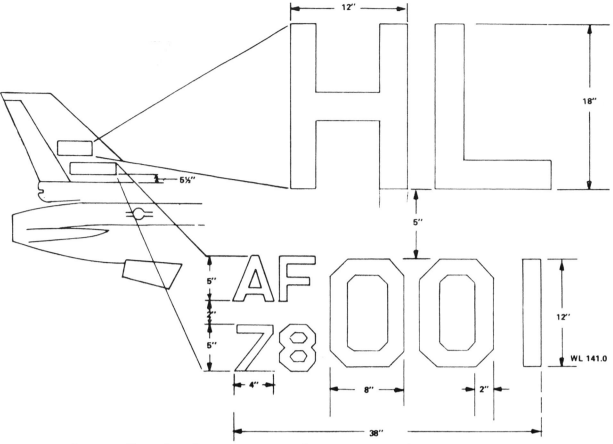

Figure D-38. DISTINCTIVE UNIT AND SERIAL NUMBER SIZES, F-16 AIRCRAFT

Figure D-39. DISTINCTIVE UNIT AND SERIAL NUMBER SIZES, UH-1F AIRCRAFT

[DISTINCTIVE UNIT MARKINGS - CODE LIST]

AK	F-15	21st TFW, Elmendorf AFB, Alaska		MD	A-10	175th TFG, Martin Airport, Maryland
AK	A-10	343d TFW, Eielson AFB, Alaska		MI	F-16	127th TFW, Selfridge ANGB, Michigan
AL	F-16	187th TFG, Dannelly Field, Alabama		MJ	F-16	432d TFW, Misawa AB, Japan
AR	A-10	10th TFW, RAF Alconbury, UK		MO	EF/F-111	366th TFW, Mountain Home AFB, Idaho
AZ	A-7, F-16	162d TFG, Tucson IAP, Arizona		MY	F-16	347th TFW, Moody AFB, Georgia
BA	RF-4	67th TRW, Bergstrom AFB, Texas		NF	OA-10	602d TACW, Davis-Monthan AFB, Arizona
BC	OA-37, A-10	110th TASG, Battle Creek ANGB, Michigan		NJ	F-4	108th TFW, McGuire AFB, New Jersey
BD	A-10	917th TFW, Barksdale AFB, Louisiana		NM	A-7	150th TFG, Kirtland AFB, New Mexico
BH	RF-4	117th TRW, Birmingham MAP, Alabama		NO	A-10	926th TFG, NAS New Orleans, Louisiana
BT	F-15	36th TFW, Bitburg AB, Germany		NT	T-43	323d FTW, Mather AFB, California
CC	F-111	27th TFW, Cannon AFB, New Mexico		NY	F-16	174th TFW, Hancock Field, New York
CO	A-7	140th TFW, Buckley ANGB, Colorado		OH	A-7	121st TFW, Rickenbacker ANGB, Ohio
CR	F-15	32d TFG, Soesterberg AB, Netherlands		OH	A-7	178th TFG, Springfield MAP, Ohio
CT	A-10	103d TFG, Bradley ANGB, Connecticut		OH	A-7	180th TFG, Toledo MAP, Ohio
DC	F-16	113th TFW, Andrews AFB, Maryland		OK	A-7	138th TFG, Tulsa IAP, Oklahoma
DM	A-10	355th TTW, Davis-Monthan AFB, Arizona		OS	F-16, A-10	51st TFW, Osan AB, Korea
DO	F-16	906th TFG, Wright-Patterson AFB, Ohio		OT	Various	TAWC, Eglin AFB, Florida
ED	Various	6510th TW, Edwards AFB, California		PA	OA-10	111th TASG, Willow Grove ARFF, Pennsylvania
EG	F-15	33rd TFW, Eglin AFB, Florida				
EL	A-10	23d TFW, England AFB, Louisiana		PR	A-7	156th TFG, Puerto Rico IAP, Puerto Rico
ET	Various	3246th TW, Eglin AFB, Florida		PT	A-7	112th TFG, Greater Pittsburgh IAP, Pennsylvania
FF	F-15, H-1, EC-135	1st TFW, Langley AFB, Virginia				
				RS	F-16	86th TFW, Ramstein AB, Germany
FM	F-16	482d TFW, Homestead AFB, Florida		SA	F-16	149th TFG, Kelly AFB, Texas
FS	F-16	188th TFW, Fort Smith MAP, Arkansas		SB	EC-130	66th ECW, Sembach AB, Germany
FW	F-4	122d TFW, Fort Wayne MAP, Indiana		SD	A-7	114th TFG, Joe Foss Field, South Dakota
GA	F-4	35th TFW, George AFB, California		SH	F-16	507th TFG, Tinker AFB, Oklahoma
GU	RF-4	460th TRG, Taegu AB, Korea		SI	F-16	183rd TFG, Springfield Airport, Illinois
HA	A-7	185th TFG, Sioux City, Iowa		SJ	F-15, KC-10	4th Wing, Seymour Johnson AFB, North Carolina
HF	F-4	181st TFG, Hulman RAP, Indiana				
HI	F-16	419th TFW, Hill AFB, Utah		SL	F-4	131st TFW, Bridgeton, Missouri
HL	F-16	388th TFW, Hill AFB, Utah		SP	F-4, F-16	52d TFW, Spangdahlem AB, Germany
HM	AT-38	479th TTW, Holloman AFB, New Mexico		SR	OV-10, OA-10	507th TACW, Shaw AFB, South Carolina
HO	F-15	49th TFW, Holloman AFB, New Mexico		SW	F-16	363d TFW, Shaw AFB, South Carolina
HR	F-16	50th TFW, Hahn AB, Germany		TF	F-16	301st TFW, Carswell AFB, Texas
HS	F-16	31st TFW, Homestead AFB, Florida		TJ	F-16	401st TFW, Torrejon AB, Spain
IA	F-16	132d TFW, Des Moines MAP, Iowa		TR	F-117	37th TFW, Tonopah Test Range, Nevada
IL	OA-37	182d TASG, Greater Peoria Airport, Illinois		TX	F-16	924th TFG, Bergstrom AFB, Texas
IN	A-10	930th TFG, Grissom AFB, Indiana		TY	F-15	325th TTW, Tyndall AFB, Florida
IS	F-15	57th FIS, NAS Keflavik, Iceland		UH	F-111	20th TFW, RAF Upper Heyford, UK
KC	A-10	442d TFW, Richards-Gebaur ANGB, Missouri		UH	EF-111	66th ECW, RAF Upper Heyford, UK
LA	F-15	405th TTW, Luke AFB, Arizona		VA	A-7	192d TFG, Byrd Field, Virginia
LF	F-16	58th TTW, Luke AFB, Arizona		WA	Various	57th FWW, Nellis AFB, Nevada
LN	F-111	48th TFW, RAF Lakenheath, UK		WI	A-10	128th TFW, Truax Field, Wisconsin
LR	F-16	944th TFG, Luke AFB, Arizona		WP	F-16	8th TFW, Kunsan AB, Korea
LY	F-15	48th FIS, Langley AFB, Virginia		WR	A-10	81st TFW, RAF Bentwaters, UK
MA	A-10	104th TFG, Barnes MAP, Massachusetts		WW	F-4	35th TFW, George AFB, California
MB	A-10	354th TFW, Myrtle Beach AFB, South Carolina		ZR	RF-4	26th TRW, Zweibrucken AB, Germany
MC	F-16	56th TTW, MacDill AFB, Florida		ZZ	F-15	18th TFW, Kadena AB, Okinawa

[All USAF flying units were contacted by the author in the preparation of this chart. All codes listed have seen use since January 1990; codes, equipment, designations, and base assignments are subject to change.]

APPENDIX E
SERVICING, GROUND HANDLING, EMERGENCY, HAZARD WARNING MARKINGS AND ARMAMENT PLACARD LOCATIONS FOR AIRCRAFT

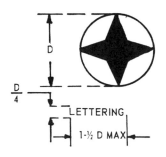

DIMENSIONS ±.05	
D	D/4
2 INCHES	1/2 INCH
4 INCHES	1 INCH

LETTERING WHICH SUPPLEMENTS THE
SYMBOLS SHALL BE IN THE SCALE 1 TO
4 IN RELATION TO THE SYMBOL.

Figure E-1. Typical Symbol Dimensioning

FILLING (a)

FUELING	FILLED FOUR POINTED STAR WITH NOTATION OF NATO CODE NUMBER FOR FUEL	(NATO CODE NO.)	**OXYGEN (BREATHING)**	TWO HORIZONTAL FILLED RECTANGLES WITH NOTATION OF EITHER "GAS" OR "LIQUID". FOR GASEOUS OXYGEN INCLUDE CHARGING PRESSURES IN ENGLISH AND METRIC UNITS. FOR LIQUID OXYGEN INCLUDE CAPACITY IN LITRES. WHEN NECESSARY. ___ psi ___ Kg/Cm^2 ___ LITRES
ROCKET FUELS	FILLED FOUR POINTED STAR IN CRESCENT WITH NOTATION OF NATO CODE NUMBER FOR ROCKET FUEL	(NATO CODE NO.)	**ANTI-DETONANT OR THRUST AUGMENTATION**	 FILLED CHEVRON WITH NOTATION OF NATO CODE NUMBER (NATO CODE NO.)
ROCKET OXIDIZER	FILLED CRESCENT WITH NOTATION OF NATO CODE NUMBER FOR ROCKET OXIDIZER	(NATO CODE NO.)	**AIR CONDITIONING**	DOT PATTERN
ENGINE LUBRICATING OIL	FILLED SQUARE WITH NOTATION OF NATO CODE NUMBER FOR ENGINE LUBRICATING OIL	(NATO CODE NO.)	**NITROGEN SERVICES**	FILLED SQUARE WITH A QUARTER ARC REMOVED FROM EACH CORNER, WITH TYPE OF GAS USED AND PRESSURE IN ENGLISH AND METRIC UNITS NITROGEN ___ psi ___ Kg/Cm^2
HYDRAULIC FLUID	FILLED CIRCLE WITH NOTATION OF NATO CODE NUMBER FOR HYDRAULIC FLUID	(NATO CODE NO.)	**FIRE EXTINGUISHING SYSTEM**	A FILLED DIAMOND WITH NOTATION SHOWING NATO CODE NUMBER (NATO CODE NO.)
DE-ICING	FILLED TRIANGLE WITH NOTATION OF NATO CODE NUMBER FOR DE-ICING FLUID	(NATO CODE NO.)	**EXTERNAL ELECTRICAL CONNECTIONS**	FILLED "E" WITH LOWER LIMB SHORTENED, STATING SERVICE AND VOLTAGE DETAILS ...SERVICING ...STARTING ETC. 28V OR 112 V DC 115/200V, 400 CYCLES
COOLANT	TWO FILLED HORIZONTAL S's WITH NOTATION OF NATO CODE NUMBER FOR COOLANT AND PERCENTAGE COMPOSITION IF NECESSARY (NATO CODE NO.) WATER ___ % SOLUBLE OIL ___ %		**GROUNDING OR EARTHING RECEPTACLE**	 A FILLED INVERTED "T" WITH TWO PARALLEL BARS UNDERNEATH WHICH DIMINISH IN SIZE GROUND (EARTH) HERE
PNEUMATIC SYSTEM	FILLED X WITH NOTATION OF MAXIMUM CHARGING PRESSURE IN ENGLISH AND METRIC UNITS MAXIMUM ___ psi ___ Kg/Cm^2		**INSPECTION OF BATTERY**	A FILLED ELECTRIC FLASH SIGN

(a) COLOR - BLACK OR WHITE ACCORDING TO BACKGROUND.

Figure E-2. Aircraft Markings, Servicing and Precautioning (Sheet 1 of 2)

FILLING

COLOR - BLACK OR WHITE ACCORDING TO BACKGROUND

PNEUMATIC STARTER CONNECTION — A FILLED X CIRCUMSCRIBED BY A FILLED RING

(d)

AF DWG 65B40317 (98749)

REFRIGERANT REPLENISHMENT — TWO FILLED TRIANGLES WITH APEXES JOINED ON HORIZONTAL CENTER LINE.

HAZARD (b)

COLOR - RED - 11136

MARK BOTH SIDES OF FUSELAGE

EXPLOSIVE ACTUATED DEVICES — RED FILLED EQUILATERAL TRIANGLE, APEX DOWN, OF THE LARGEST PRACTICABLE SIZE UP TO A 9 INCH (23 cm) SIZE TO BE APPLIED TO THE EXTERNAL PART OF AIRCRAFT ADJACENT TO THE EXPLOSIVE DEVICE. THE WORD "DANGER" TO BE WITH ITS TOP TO A SURROUNDING PERIPHERAL RED LINE

DANGER DANGER DANGER

ALTERNATIVE MARKING FOR T-37/T-38 AIRCRAFT IS A WHITE EQUILATERAL TRIANGLE, APEX DOWN, 9 INCHES HIGH WHICH INCLUDES A 1/4 INCH RED BORDER. THE WORD 'DANGER' AND EXPLANATORY TEXT IS PRINTED IN RED ON THE WHITE BACKGROUND.

DANGER THIS AIRPLANE CONTAINS EJECTION SEATS, CANOPY REMOVERS AND EXPLOSIVE CHARGES. SEE T.O.-2 FOR INSTRUCTIONS.

GROUND HANDLING

b

COLOR - ORANGE-YELLOW - 13538

JACKING POINT — ORANGE YELLOW FILLED SQUARE WITH TWO SLANTING LEGS ON BOTTOM SIDE

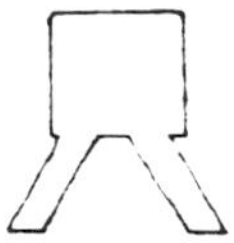

(d)

AF DWG 65B40297 (98749)

SLINGING OR HOISTING POINTS — ORANGE YELLOW FILLED HOOK ON A HORIZONTAL LINE

(d)

AF DWG 65B40294 (98749)

MOORING OR PICKETING — ORANGE YELLOW FILLED ANCHOR

(d)

AF DWG 65B40295 (98749)

TOWING (c) — ORANGE YELLOW FILLED RING

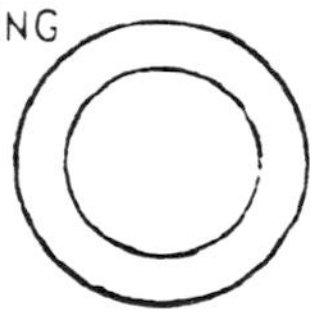

(c)

AF DWG 65B40296 (98749)

AIRBORNE AUXILIARY TURBINE POWER PLANT INLET AND OR EXHAUST

COLOR CODE

RED

BLACK

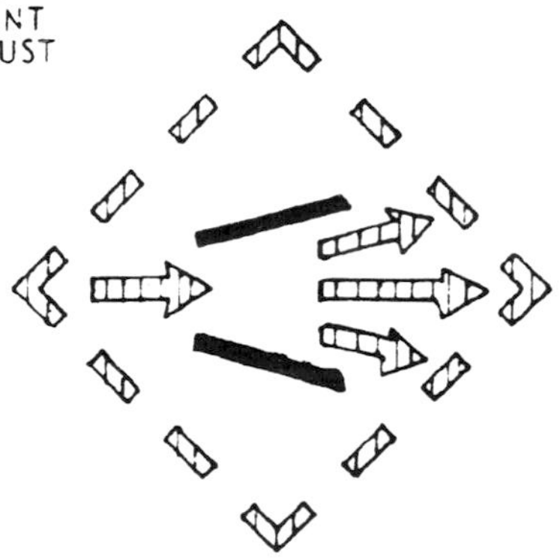

(d)

AF DWG 65B40320 (98749)

(b) OUTLINE SYMBOLS IN BLACK OR WHITE ACCORDING TO THE BACKGROUND.
(c) OPTIONAL WHERE TOWING POINT IS OBVIOUS AND SUITABLE LOCATION FOR SYMBOL IS NOT AVAILABLE.
(d) OFFICE OF PRIMARY RESPONSIBILITY (OPR) 2852 ABG DAPT, McCLELLAN AFB CA 95652-5000

Figure E-2. Aircraft Markings, Servicing and Precautioning (Sheet 2 of 2)

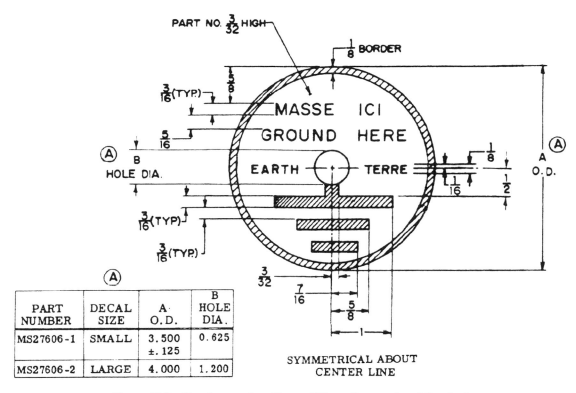

Figure E-3. Decalcomania - Ground Here, International Symbol.

PART NUMBER	DECAL SIZE	A. O.D.	B HOLE DIA.
MS27606-1	SMALL	3.500 ±.125	0.625
MS27606-2	LARGE	4.000	1.200

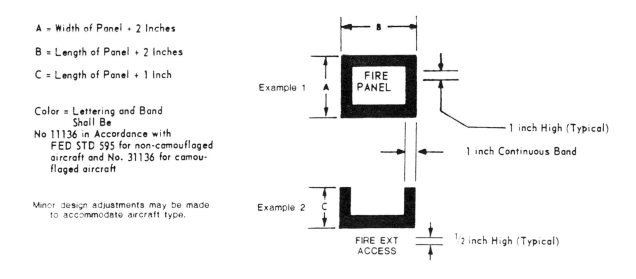

A = Width of Panel + 2 Inches

B = Length of Panel + 2 Inches

C = Length of Panel + 1 Inch

Color = Lettering and Band
    Shall Be
No 11136 in Accordance with
  FED STD 595 for non-camouflaged
  aircraft and No. 31136 for camouflaged aircraft

Minor design adjustments may be made
  to accommodate aircraft type.

Figure E-4. Markings for Fire Access Panel

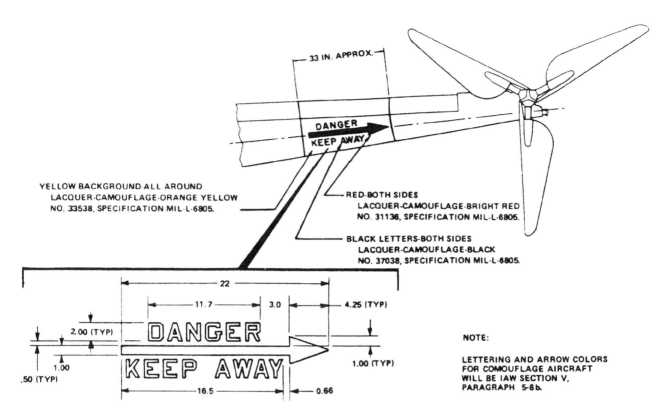

Figure E-5. Helicopter Tail Boom Markings

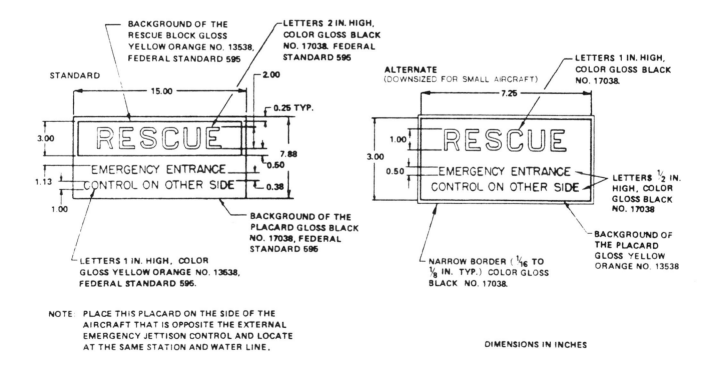

Figure E-6. Emergency Instruction Markings

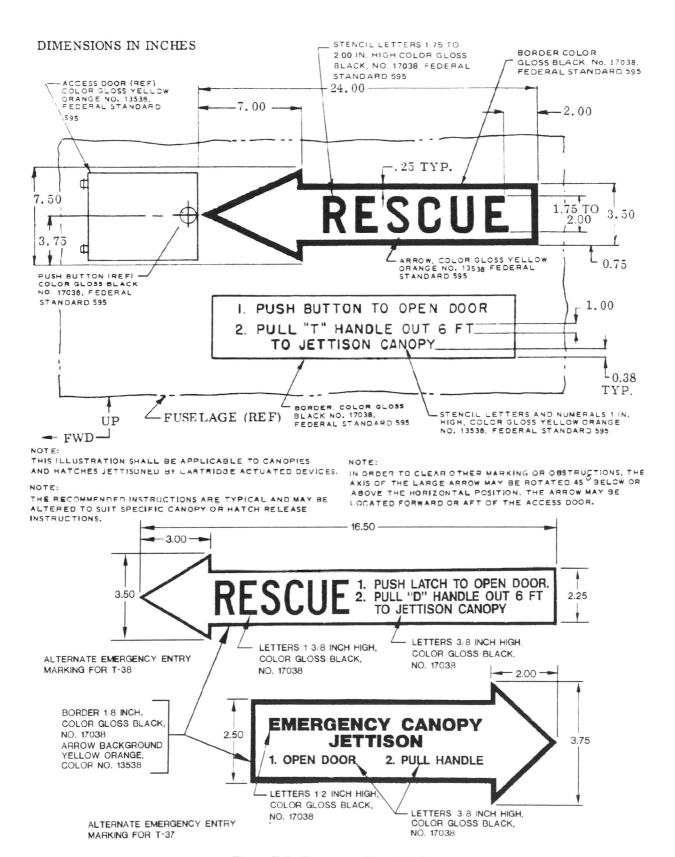

Figure E-7. Emergency Entry Markings

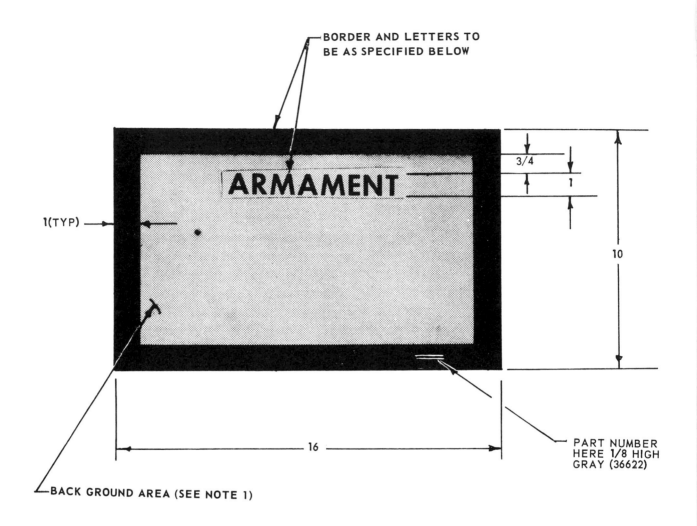

ORDER DECALS OR APPLY PAINT APPROPRIATELY AS FOLLOWS:

COLORS

	BACKGROUND		BORDER & LETTERING
−1	GRAY (36622)	CAMOUFLAGE	BLACK (37038)
−2	TAN (30219)	CAMOUFLAGE	BLACK (37038)
−3	GREEN (34079)	CAMOUFLAGE	BLACK (37038)
−4	GREEN (34102)	CAMOUFLAGE	BLACK (37038)
−5	WHITE (17875)	NON-CAMOUFLAGE	RED (11136)
−6	BLACK (17038)	CAMOUFLAGE	RED (11136)
-7	WHITE (17875)	CAMOUFLAGE	YELLOW (13538)

NOTES:

1. PLACARD ON CAMOUFLAGE A/C
   TO HAVE SAME COLOR BACKGROUND
   AS THE AREA TO WHICH APPLIED.

2. COLOR NUMBERS PER
   FED-STD 595

Figure E-8. Armament Placard Marking

128

TYPE AIRCRAFT	PLACARD LOCATIONS
A-7/A-7D	Locate decal immediately below panel 1222-10 and to the left of panel 1222-9. Placement will be such that the decal is horizontal to the ramp surface.
A-37	Locate decal on the left side of the aircraft between stations 54.00 and 78.20, with the upper edge placed one inch below the strake mounting bracket and the right edge running parallel to the cockpit entrance step.
B-52	Locate decal on left hand forward fuselage at station 315.50 to 331.50, 23 to 33 inches below WL139, measuring along skin contour.
HC-130	Locate the decal on left hand side of fuselage so trailing edge of placard is five inches in front of crew entrance door and the top of the placard is three inches below the top of the door.
MC-130	Locate placard on the left side of aircraft with the leading edge of the placard 14 inches aft of the crew entrance door, and with the top edge of the placard 24 inches below the top edge of the door.
RF/F-4	Locate the decal on the outboard surface of the left intake duct of panel 125L, so as not to be covered when engine covers are installed.
F-111A/E/D/F & FB-111A	Locate decal on crew module forward access panel 1208, 1.5 inches from lower edge and 8.5 inches from aft edge.
UH-1F/N	Locate decal between station 74.25 and station 64.25, 18 inches above the door sill.
UH-1N	Locate decal on door post, aft of pilot's door.
H-3	Center decal on panel below window of personnel door.
H-53	Locate decal on right-hand side of fuselage forward of personnel door, between stations 162 and 182, WL120.
UH-60A	Locate placard on the right side personnel door, centered four inches below the forward window.
T-38	Locate decal even with the trailing edge of the LOX servicing door and parallel to the bottom of the door.
OV-10A	Locate decal on the right side of the aircraft between fuselage station 4288 and 60.60, vertically two inches above top edge of right fuselage access panel part No. 300-310021-6.

Figure E-9. Armament Placard Locations

[This chart has been modified by the deletion of obsolete aircraft.]

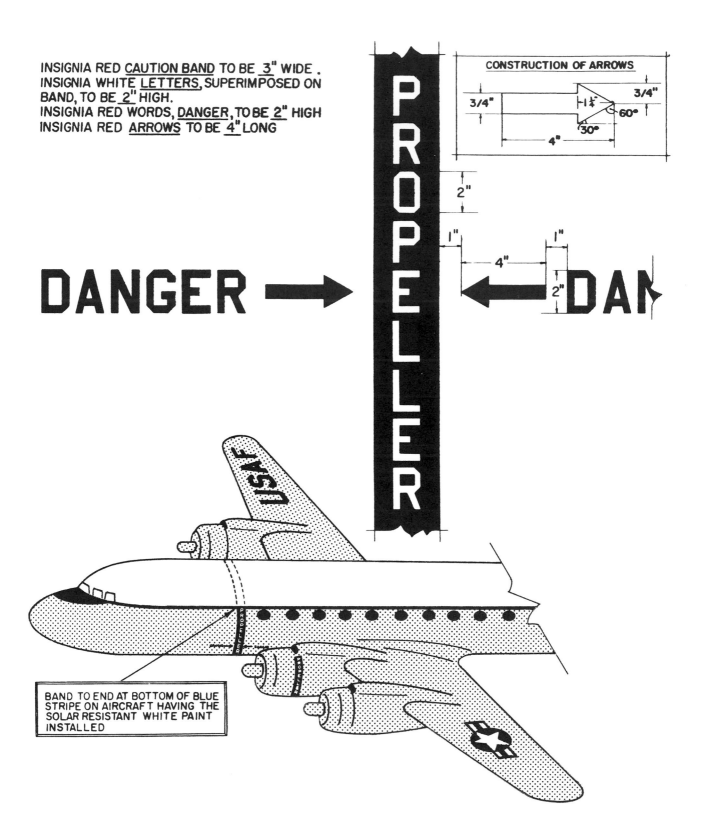

INSIGNIA RED <u>CAUTION BAND</u> TO BE 3" WIDE .
INSIGNIA WHITE <u>LETTERS</u>, SUPERIMPOSED ON
BAND, TO BE 2" HIGH.
INSIGNIA RED WORDS, <u>DANGER</u>, TO BE 2" HIGH
INSIGNIA RED <u>ARROWS</u> TO BE 4" LONG

CONSTRUCTION OF ARROWS

BAND TO END AT BOTTOM OF BLUE
STRIPE ON AIRCRAFT HAVING THE
SOLAR RESISTANT WHITE PAINT
INSTALLED

Figure E-10. Propeller Warning Stripes and Signs

130

APPENDIX F

IDENTIFICATION CODES AND MARKINGS

FOR TUBING, HOSE, AND PIPE FOR

AIRCRAFT

F-1. <u>Colors.</u> Colors conforming to FED-STD-595 as indicated below shall be used to denote function.

Color	FED-STD-595 Code No.
Blue	15102
Green	14187
Yellow	13655
Orange	12197
Red	11136
Brown	10049
Gray	16473
Black	17038

F-2. <u>Application Colors.</u> Color coding shall be based upon function as indicated below. Where more than one color is required to identify a single function the order of colors is from left to right, and the colored area shall be composed of vertical stripes, of equal width, of the required colors (see Figures F-2 and F-4).

Function	Color
Fuel	Red
Rocket Oxidizer	Green, Gray
Rocket Fuel	Red, Gray
Water Injection	Red, Gray, Red
Lubrication	Yellow
Hydraulic	Blue, Yellow
Solvent	Blue, Brown
Pneumatic Air	Orange, Blue
Instrument Air	Orange, Gray
Coolant	Blue
Breathing Oxygen	Green
Air Conditioning	Brown, Gray
Monopropellant	Yellow, Orange
Battery Activator	Yellow, Gray
Rain Repellents	Blue, Gray
Vacuum	Gray, Orange, Gray
Fire Protection	Brown
De-Icing	Gray
Rocket Catalyst	Yellow, Green
Compressed Gas	Orange
Electrical Conduit	Brown, Orange
Inerting Fluid	Orange, Green

F-3. <u>Designation of hazards.</u> Hazardous materials or conditions shall be designated in black letters on white or metallic (silvery or chrome) background as specified below (see Figure F-1). Where such hazards result from working pressure only, and where the pressure is indicated in the identification, no further identification of hazard is necessary. Under conditions warranting special care over and above that required for the identified hazard, the skull-and-cross-bones symbol, illustrated in Figure F-3, shall be used.

F-4. Hazards. Hazards shall be identified in accordance with above letter sizes [and] shall be the same as those used for function within the same identification group, with a 1/32-inch vertical space between words comprising a set, i.e., a dual hazard, and a 1/4-inch space between sets (or between words if only a single hazard is indicated). Where tapes are used to identify function, identification of hazard may be accomplished with tape(s) of 1/2-inch minimum width. When painted or appearing on tags or bands the hazard shall be the last word(s) in the identification following the direction-of-flow arrow, if applicable. Hazards associated with various line contents shall be in accordance with primary and secondary warning designations as established in MIL-STD-101. However, for application under this technical manual, words and abbreviations are to be substituted for colors to identify specific classes of hazards as indicated under "identification Marking" below. To facilitate cross-referencing, MIL-STD-101 colors applicable to all hazards are indicated opposite the identification markings. Thus it will only be necessary to refer to the color shown in Table II of MIL-STD-101 for a particular content, then substitute applicable words or abbreviations.

CLASS OF HAZARD	IDENTIFICATION MARKING	MIL-STD-101 COLOR
Flammable materials. All materials known ordinarily as flammable or combustibles.	FLAM-----------	Yellow
Toxic and poisonous materials. All materials extremely hazardous to life or health, under normal conditions, as toxic or poisons.	TOXIC-----------	Brown
Anaesthetics and harmful materials. All materials productive or anaesthetic vapors and all liquid chemicals and compounds hazardous to life and property but not normally productive of dangerous quantities of fumes or vapors.	AAHM------------	Blue
Oxidizing materials. All materials which readily furnish oxygen for combustion and fire producers which react explosively or with evolution of heat in contact with any other materials.	OXYM------------	Green
Physically dangerous materials. All materials, not dangerous in themselves, which are asphyxiating in confined areas or which are generally handled in a dangerous physical state pressure or temperature.	PHDAN-----------	Gray
Fire protection materials. All materials provided in piping systems or in compressed gas cylinders exclusively for use in fire protection.	FPM-------------	Red

FUNCTION	SYMBOL	ILLUSTRATION
ROCKET OXIDIZER	CRESCENT	
ROCKET CATALYST	VERTICAL STRIPES	
ROCKET FUEL	FOUR-POINT STAR INSIDE CRESCENT	
FUEL	FOUR-POINT STAR	
WATER INJECTION	INVERTED CHEVRONS	
LUBRICATION	STAGGERED SQUARES	
HYDRAULIC	CIRCLE	
COMPRESSED GAS	BROAD DIAGONAL STRIPE	
INSTRUMENT AIR	CONTINUOUS ZIG-ZAG LINE	
COOLANT	HORIZONTALS	
BREATHING OXYGEN	RECTANGLE	
AIR CONDITIONING	GRAVEL PATTERN	
FIRE PROTECTION	HORIZONTAL DIAMOND	
DE-ICING	STAGGERED TRIANGLES	
PNEUMATIC	CONTINUOUS X-FORM LATTICE	
ELECTRICAL CONDUIT	FLASH OF LIGHTNING	
INERTING FLUID	STAGGERED PIPE CROSSES	
SOLVENT	HORIZONTAL STRIPES	
MONOPROPELLANT	BLOCK T	
VACUUM	VERTICAL WAVY LINE	
BATTERY ACTIVATOR	SPARKLING	
RAIN REPELLENT	RAIN DROPS	

Table F-1. Functions and Associated Symbols

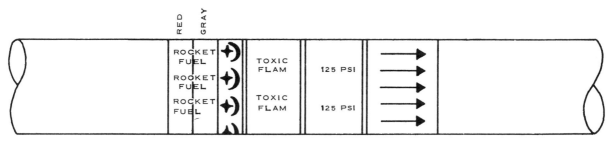

IDENTIFICATION GROUP USING TAPES

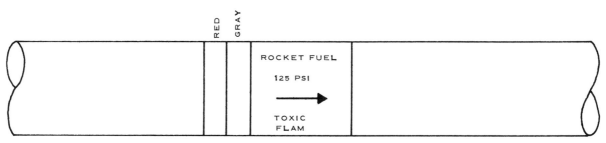

IDENTIFICATION GROUP USING PAINTS

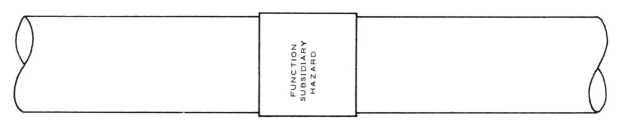

IDENTIFICATION GROUP USING BAND NAS 1411

Figure F-1. Examples of Identification Groups

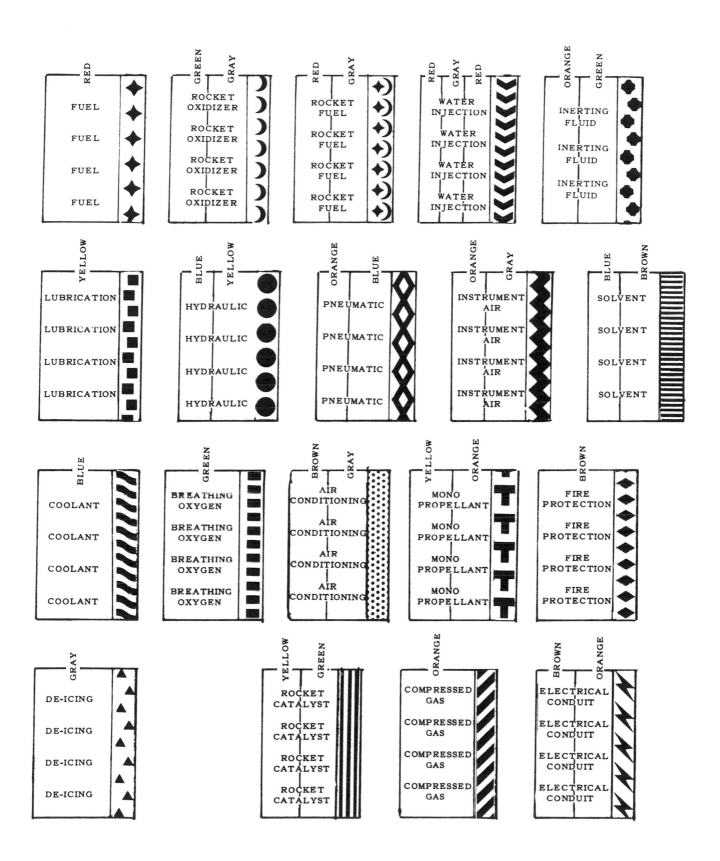

Figure F-2. Color-coded Functional Identification Tapes (Sheet 1 of 2)

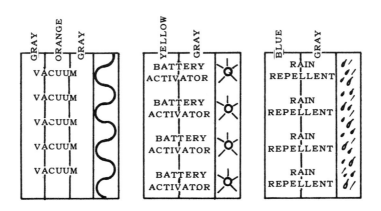

Figure F-2. Color-coded Functional Identification Tapes (Sheet 2 of 2)

1. Warning symbols to be printed on tapes.

2. Maximum width of tape 1/2 inch. Clearance between the symbol and the edge of the tape on either side, shall be approximately one-fourth the width of the symbol.

3. Symbol to be black on a white or metallic (silvery or chrome) background.

4. Symbols shall recur at a maximum interval of 1/4 inch.

5. This symbol should be used sparingly and should not be used on lines to warn against high pressure, or against a hazard already identified.

6. The warning symbol shall be placed immediately adjacent to the identification group at the end opposite the functional tape.

NOTE: This symbol may be stenciled on tags and painted bands, or stamped on aluminum alloy tags.

Figure F-3. Warning Symbols

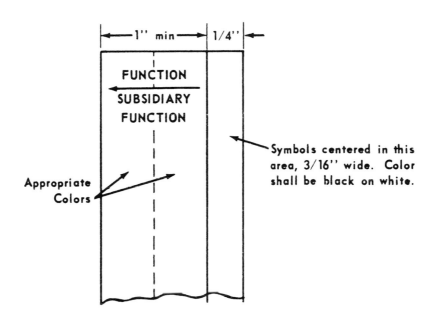

NOTES:

1. Letters shall be printed in black, 3/32" high with 1/32" between lines of a legend and 1/4" between a legend and its repetition.

2. Arrow shall be black, head 3/32" high, and shaft 1/32" wide.

3. Arrow to have head on both ends for reversible flow.

4. Colors shall conform to paragraph F-2 and Symbols as shown in table F-1.

5. Tape shall be a minimum of 1" wide.

Figure F-4. Optional Arrangement for Identification

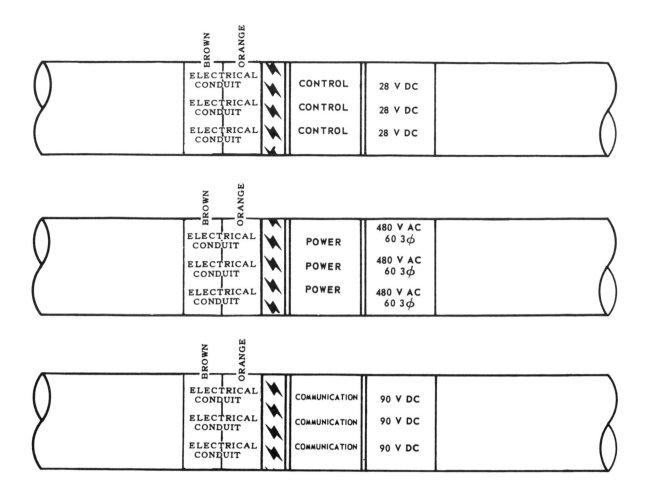

Figure F-5. Examples of Electrical Identification

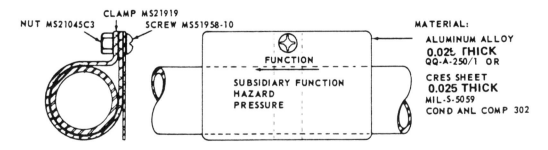

NOTES: 1. Tag sizes shall be compatible with the diameter of the tubing.

2. Size of letters for wording on tag shall be compatible with tag.

3. Arrow size shall be compatible with letters.

4. Arrow shall have head on both ends for reversible flow.

5. If temperature exceeds 500°F or if tags are used on LOX lines, remove cushion from clamp and use plain clamp.

6. More than one clamp may be used if required for rigidity.

Figure F-6. Tag Identification

[APPENDIX G]

[GLOSSARY]

ABW	Air Base Wing
AFLC	AF Logistics Command (merging with AFSC in 1992 to form AF Materiel Command)
AFSC	AF Systems Command (merging with AFLC in 1992 to form AF Materiel Command)
AFR	Air Force Regulation
AFRES	Air Force Reserve
AFSOC	Air Force Special Operations Command
aliphatic	organic compounds in which carbon atoms link in open chains rather than rings.
ALD	Air Lift Division
ANG	Air National Guard
ARRS	Air Rescue and Recovery Service, which became Air Rescue Service on 1 August 1989. When used as a unit designation (e.g., "67th ARRS") the abbreviation stands for Air Rescue and Recovery <u>Squadron</u>. These squadrons were redesignated Air Rescue Squadrons when the ARS was organized.
ARS	Air Rescue Service (see ARRS). When used as a unit designation (e.g., "20th ARS") the abbreviation stands for Air Rescue <u>Squadron</u>.
AW	Airlift Wing
AWACW	Airborne Warning and Control Wing
CONUS	Continental United States - usually referring to the original 48 states; sometimes also including Alaska and Hawaii.
MAAG	Military Assistance Advisory Group
MAC	Military Airlift Command (to be replaced by Air Mobility Command by the mid-1990s)
MAJCOM	Major Command. MAJCOMs are the highest decision-making levels beneath Hq USAF.
MAS/MAG/MAW	Military Airlift Squadron, Military Airlift Group, Military Airlift Wing
PACAF	Pacific Air Forces
PMRT	Program Management Responsibility Transfer
SAC	Strategic Air Command (scheduled to merge most of its combat assets with TAC to form Air Combat Command by the mid-1990s)
SEA	South-East Asia; during the 1960s and '70s used interchangeably with "Vietnam War."
SM-ALC	Sacramento Air Logistics Center, located at McClellan AFB, California.
SOS	Special Operations Squadron
Special Missions/ Special Operations	In the USAF Special Mission organizations are charged with transportation of Presidential, Congressional, diplomatic, and command-level personnel - what the press would call "VIPs." Special Operations organizations prepare for unconventional warfare, direct actions. special reconnaissance, counterterrorism, and foreign internal defense - all "air commando" missions. Aircraft paint schemes for these are applied appropriately.
TAC	Tactical Air Command (scheduled to merge most of its combat assets with SAC to form Air Combat Command by the mid-1990s)
USAFE	US Air Forces in Europe
WR-ALC	Warner-Robins Air Logistics Center, located at Robins AFB, Georgia

[APPENDIX H]

[COLOR LISTING]

US Military colors are usually documented in Federal Standard 595, the US catalog of standard colors used by various Government departments. The branches of the military were able to include the colors from their own standards when FS 595 was first assembled in 1956, and have added many new colors in the thirty-five years since.

Individual colors are sometimes named unofficially, but FS 595 identifies each color by a five digit number. The first digit describes the gloss, with "1" for gloss, "2" for semi-gloss, and "3" for lusterless. The second digit classifies the predominant color value, with "0" for browns, "1" for reds, "2" for oranges, "3" for yellows, "4" for greens, "5" for blues, "6" for grays, "7" for miscellaneous colors (including black, white, and metallics), and "8" for fluorescents. The remaining three digits group colors within each classification group from darkest to lightest. The last three digits meaning beyond identification - No. 34083 is not "halfway" between 34082 and 34084; nor is 34090 related in any way to 31090.

Within the USAF, color schemes are approved at Major Command (MAJCOM) level, which is one reason so many color scheme variations have been employed. The first USAF multiple-color camouflage approved in 1964 soon had a SAC variation using different colors. Likewise the European I camouflage employed by TAC during the 1980s had its own MAC variation; F-4s and A-7s flew with other modifications of the scheme. Even in the 1990s, with SAC and TAC settling independently on one gray for their monochromatic schemes, MAC independently arrived at a different gray.

Some of the common standard camouflage schemes used since the 1960s:

Standard TAC (1960s/70s)	Tan 30219	Green 34102	Green 34079	Gray 36622 Undersides
TAC SEA Scheme (1960s/70s)	Tan 30219	Green 34102	Green 34079	Black 17038 Undersides
Standard SAC (1960s/70s)	"Tan" 34201	Green 34159	Green 34079	White 17875 Undersides
SAC SEA Scheme (1960s/70s)	"Tan" 34201	Green 34159	Green 34079	Black 17038 Undersides
Asia Minor Scheme (not used)	Tan 20400	Brown 30140	Green 34079	Gray 36622 Undersides
European I (1980s)	Gray 36081	Green 34092	Green 34102	(Wraparound)
European I (MAC)(1980s)	Gray 36118	Green 34092	Green 34102	(Wraparound on helicopters, 36118 undersides on transports)

Strategic Camouflage (1980s) Gray 36118 below Green 34086 Above Gray 36081 Wraparound

The following listing describes the commonly used color numbers stocked by the USAF:

30140   Listed as "Brown Special," 30140 was one of three upper surface colors standardized for the Asia Minor camouflage scheme, a scheme which was not used operationally by the USAF. During Operation Desert Storm, 30140 was used on USAF helicopters with 20400 in a modified Asia Minor scheme.

30219   Originated by the Navy (BuShips to match BuDocks No. 5 Medium Tan Lustreless), 30219 became the tan in TAC's standard camouflage of 1960s/70s. The color is falling out of use as camouflage systems are revised; by the beginning of the 1990s, F-111's were the only USAF aircraft using 30219.

30266	Based on WWII color ANA 615, the RAF's Middle Stone. The color was used for propeller tips during the 1950s and (as "Tan Special") for a unique C-130 Desert scheme (see page 93) in the 1980s. By the early 1990s use of the scheme and the color had all but ended.
20400	Listed as "Tan Special," 20400 was one of three upper surface colors standardized for the Asia Minor camouflage scheme, a scheme which was not used operationally by the USAF. During Operation Desert Storm, 20400 was used on USAF helicopters with 30140 in a modified Asia Minor scheme.
11136, 21136, 31136	Insignia Red. The FS 595 color was based on ANA 509 Insignia Red. The most commonly used red in the USAF, Insignia Red appears in the National Star Insignia and warning markings. The color has also been used for arctic markings.
12197	International Orange. Based on ANA 508 International Orange. 12197 would be the standard color for USAF conspicuity and Arctic markings if the Air Force was currently using these markings. 12197 is still in use as the color for target drones. (12197 does not appear in the color chip chart at the end of this book.)
13538, 33538	Originated as BuShips Paint, Striping, Yellow Formula No. 42. This is the standard orange-yellow used for warning and rescue markings.
33722	The only USAF use of 33722 came in the 1980s as "Creme Special" in MAC's C-130 desert scheme (see page 93).
34079	Based on US Army Corps of Engineers Forest Green. 34079 was once one of the most widely-used USAF camouflage colors but operational use of the color will end by the mid-1990s. During the 1960s and '70s 34079 was the one common color in the standard TAC and SAC camouflage schemes; it was also specified for the USAF's Asia Minor scheme. At this writing it can be found only on F-111s and a few B-52s and F-4Es.
34086	34086 came to FS 595 from TT-C-595 color No. 3403. Similar to the USAAF's WWII Dark Olive Drab, 34086 has seen brief use in SAC's recent Strategic Camouflage Scheme for B-1s, B-52s, and FB-111s.
34092	Originated as BuShips Paint, Deck, Dark Green Formula No. 19 (perhaps related to ANA 612). Since the late 1970s, this has been the dark green in the standard MAC and TAC European I camouflage schemes.
34102	Based on US Army Corps of Engineers Dark Green. 34102 was the lighter of the two greens in the standard TAC camouflage of the 1960s and '70s. It is still used in the standard MAC and TAC European I camouflage schemes.
34159	34159 originated with BuShips as BuDocks No. 12 Spruce Green. This was the middle green in the SAC camouflage which originated in the 1960s.
34201	From BuShips as Nav-Ord Light Olive. Although often listed as "tan," 34201 was the lightest green in the original SAC camouflage.
15044, 25044 35044	Insignia Blue. Derived from ANA 502 (or 605, flat) Insignia Blue. It is used for National Star Insignia and USAF markings. It is the blue in ATC's blue & white trainer scheme for T-37s, and is used by the 1st Helicopter Squadron in a special mission scheme for UH-1Ns.
35231	35231 has only one known USAF use: it is the color of the horizontal fuselage stripe on the E-4. (35231 does not appear in the color chip chart at the end of this book.)
35237	Although 35237 is a major color on the Navy's camouflage pallet, its USAF use was limited to a brief stint as the grayish blue for anti-glare and markings on the EF-111. (35237 does not appear in the color chip chart at the end of this book.)
BAC 5070	The darker of two Boeing Aircraft Co. blues used exclusively by the 89th AW for Special Missions aircraft. The color is also purchased as DuPont Series 1000 826X638.

BAC 5071   The lighter of two Boeing Aircraft Co. blues used exclusively by the 89th AW for Special Missions aircraft. The color is also purchased as DuPont Series 1000 826X634.

35526   Originated as Navy Yards & Docks 10 Light Blue. 35526 was the sky blue used in the C-130 desert scheme (see page 93).

36081   Originated as ANA 513 Engine Gray. 36081 is the dark gray in TAC's European I scheme and the darker gray in the SAC Strategic Camouflage Scheme. It is the upper surface color on camouflaged KC-10s and KC-135s. It has also been used as the overall color for the monochromatic B-52 scheme (now being replaced by 36118).

26118, 36118   The once and future color! Originated as BuShips Formula No. 11, No. 109 (related to ANA 603 Sea Gray, the replacement for WWII Neutral Gray). In the early 1970s 36118 became Gunship Gray, used overall on AC-130s. By the 1980s it had become the gray in MAC's European I scheme, the dark gray on F-16 upper surfaces, and the standard overall color for PACAF FACs. In the late 1980s its was added to A-7s in the (semi-gloss) gray scheme, it was the light gray in SAC's Strategic Camouflage Scheme, and it was beginning to be used overall for interdiction aircraft such as the F-15E and the F-111. In 1991 SAC began using the color overall for its B-52s and B-1s.

36173   Originated as BuShips Formula 17, No. 50. Announced as overall color for MAC's heavy airlifters during the summer of 1991; semi-gloss formula may be used instead.

36176   Originated as Nav-Ord Ocean Gray. Used by PACAF as the darker gray for the new F-15 "Mod Eagle" scheme.

36231   Originated as ANA 621 Dark Gull Gray. Only USAF listing for C-130 wing-walk area. (36231 does not appear in the color chip chart at the end of this book.)

36251   Originated as BuDocks No. 19, Light Navy Gray. Used by PACAF as the light gray in the new F-15 "Mod Eagle" scheme.

26270 36270   Originated as BuShips Color No. 27. Used as the medium gray on F-16 sides and (semi-gloss) as the lighter gray on the two-tone gray A-7 scheme.

36320   Dark Ghost Gray, also called Dark Compass Ghost Gray. The darker color on the standard F-15 air superiority scheme. Also used as the top surface color for EC-130s and EF-111s. Approved in 1991 as the overall color for SAC's tanker force.

36375   Light Ghost Gray, also called Light Compass Ghost Gray. The underside and countershading color on standard air superiority F-15s and F-16s.

36440   Originated as ANA 620 Light Gull Gray. Only USAF listing as color for OV-10 walkway border. (36440 does not appear in the color chip chart at the end of this book.)

16473 36473   Originated as ANA 512 Aircraft Gray. Aircraft Gray is the standard overall aircraft color for uncamouflaged USAF aircraft. A matt version of the color was used in the 1960s as "Counter-Insurgency Gray.)

36492   Originated as Yards & Docks No. 9 Pearl Gray. Used as the undersurface and side gray for the electronic warfare EF-111 and EC-130.

16515   Originated as Boeing Gray color No. 707, DuPont Series 1000 822x508. Often substituted for No. 16473 as the overall aircraft color (on E-3s and C-9Cs, for example).

36622   During the 1960s and early '70s, 36622 was the standard gray for undersurfaces of aircraft camouflaged in the standard TAC & Asia Minor camouflages. With the advent of wraparound schemes in the late 1970s, 36622 quickly fell out of use. (36622 does not appear in the color chip chart at the end of this book.)

17038, Originated as ANA 622 Jet Black. Used for black markings, night camouflage, and antiglare panels.
27038 (Black does not appear in the color chip chart at the end of this book.)
37038

17043 Gold Leaf. Used as an accent color on special mission aircraft. (No chip appears in the color chip chart at the end of this book.)

17178 Aluminum paint. Used for landing gear struts, etc. (No chip appears in the color chart at the end of this book.)

17875 Insignia White. Used in the National Star Insignia, SAC anti-flash painting, ATC trainers, "White
27875 cap" solar finishes, and overall special mission aircraft. Surprisingly, Insignia White is more of a pale
37875 blue-gray than white.

17925 A whiter white. Currently listed as the interior color for C-5 wheel wells.

INDEX OF AIRCRAFT TYPES

USAF
Color Chip Chart

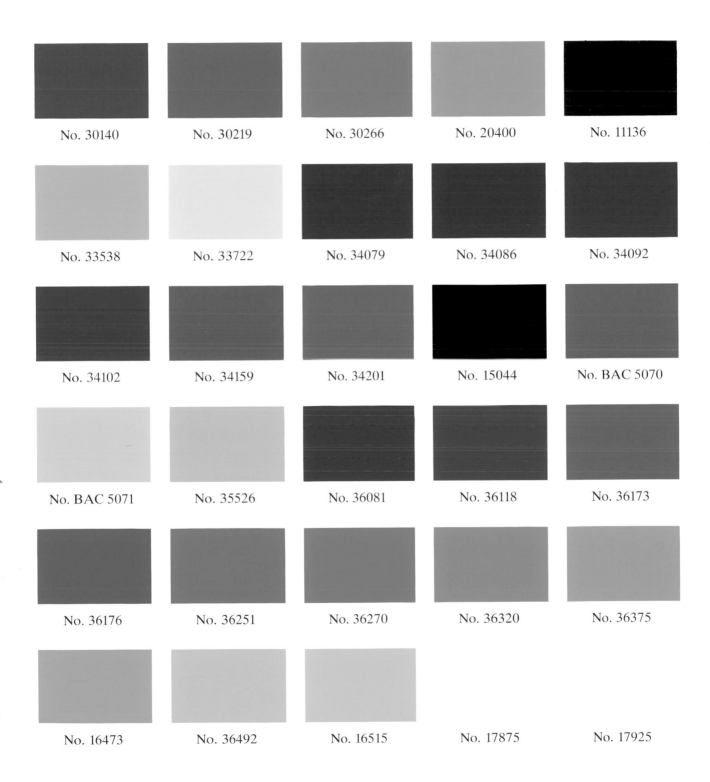

No. 30140   No. 30219   No. 30266   No. 20400   No. 11136

No. 33538   No. 33722   No. 34079   No. 34086   No. 34092

No. 34102   No. 34159   No. 34201   No. 15044   No. BAC 5070

No. BAC 5071   No. 35526   No. 36081   No. 36118   No. 36173

No. 36176   No. 36251   No. 36270   No. 36320   No. 36375

No. 16473   No. 36492   No. 16515   No. 17875   No. 17925